Dr. Melissa Tate-Scruse

Dr. Melissa Tate-Scruse

Blessed Passenger
By Dr. Melissa Tate-Scruse

Copyright @ 2018 by Dr. Melissa Tate-Scruse
Published by MediTate & Mingle
DBA Dr. Melissa Tate-Scruse

For permission requests, please direct all inquiries to:
BlindPassenger2015@gmail.com

For more information visit
www.DrMETate.com

Unless otherwise indicated, all scripture quotations are from the New King James and New Living Translations of the *Holy Bible*.

Book Design by Dr. Melissa Tate-Scruse
Cover Design by 12/24 Media LLC
Photo Image (Front Cover)
by Profound House Photography

Published in the Unites States of America
ISBN: 0692095853
ISBN-13: 978-0692095850

TABLE OF CONTENTS

Blessed Passenger

Dr. Melissa Tate-Scruse

INTRODUCTION

From Blind to Blessed

I was not brought up in church.

As the youngest of three children, and only girl, raised by childhood sweethearts, Sam and Mable, who have been married for almost fifty years. They are fun-loving, kind, and moral people, but by the time I was born they were all churched out. They were turned off by the hypocrisy of church-goers and leaders who put on their best show Sunday morning, yet continued to live foul, without rebuke, Sunday afternoon through the wee hours of late Saturday night and Sunday morning before church. I was raised to know there is a God, and I attended a sporadic church service or vacation bible study with friends or extended family; but my understanding of Him was reduced to a few limited interpretations.

First and foremost, *The Golden Rule*: Do unto others as you would have them do unto you. My aunt Gerri (affectionately nicknamed Socrates by my brother KJ) is full of wisdom and philosophical thoughts. She often threw this phrase at us as young people when someone was being spiteful or nasty. I was well into young adulthood before I realized this was an authentic biblical statement since it was easily accompanied by the not-so-biblical "God don't like ugly."

Second, *Footprints*. Visiting family in New Jersey from Maryland meant spending the night at my Aunt Cat's house. She was a church-going woman, twenty years older than my mother, with the customary plaque of *Footprints* on the wall. In the '70s, I think everybody's auntie or grandma had a plaque of *Footprints* on the wall—right next to a picture of Jesus, Martin Luther King, and wooden spoon/fork. I'm not sure how and why that became the décor of choice in black homes across America, but I vividly remember reading the poem time after time. The definitive message: God is present during all your triumphs, trials, and tribulations, even when you feel alone.

Third, *The Ten Commandments*. My mother watched the seasonal television presentation of *The Ten Commandments* every Easter. I remember watching Moses talk to the burning bush, part the Red Sea, and perform miracles to the tune of God's voice. It is a part of the greatest story ever told, but I did not understand how it was relevant to me. It certainly sparked a curiosity in me about God. I remember asking my mother if I could read the bible as I was seeking to understand what was happening in the movie—a bible I still own to this day. As a child of four or five years, I had a small scroll on my bedroom wall of a child kneeling to pray before bedtime. It read: "Now I lay me down to sleep, I pray to Lord my soul to keep. If I should die before I wake, I pray to Lord my soul to take." Beyond these circumstances, I was not raised to have a relationship with God. I did not understand the significance of prayer, except before I went to bed and before we ate dinner on special occasions. I spent far more time at bowling alleys, track meets, and football/basketball games and recreational practices than I did in any church.

It wasn't until I was twenty-two years old and married to the son a pastor, that I attended church with any regularity and intrinsic desire. I was pregnant with my first child and hundreds of miles away from home, living in a very toxic, emotional rollercoaster type of relationship. This relationship in no way resembled the childhood love story and family togetherness my parents exemplified over the years. My husband was inconsistent in his thoughts, easily agitated over the slightest things. From one day to the next, sometimes one hour to the next, you weren't quite sure what you were going to get. Something as simple as greeting him at the front door could become a major point of contention. On Monday I might hear, *"I haven't seen you all day. How come you didn't come greet me as I was coming in the door."* Whereas Tuesday was a different story, *"I'm just getting home from work and I can barely get in the door before you're in my face."* With that deep, gruff tone of voice and nasty attitude, I didn't know whether I was coming or going. His jealous rage and aggression was unpredictable—jealous because another man was checking me out or because I "liked the baby more than him." I found myself walking on eggshells, catering to his mood swings just to keep the peace.

Attending my father-in-law's church was a haven. I didn't have a voice for what I was going through, struggling with depression and feelings of shame about my marriage. No one fully understood the abrupt mood swings that were hurled in my direction. I bottled everything inside, embarrassed about it all. I felt stuck, unable to talk about my marital woes—losing myself in the process. I was no longer the fun-loving person I was raised to be. But I was faithfully attending church, having more conversations with God than ever before—far more than "now I lay me down to sleep." It was more like, "Lord please lift my spirits, deliver me from sadness, touch my husband's heart, and bring me peace!" I gave my life to Him at that church in Atlanta, but eventually fled that marriage with very little in my arms beyond my infant child. I returned to the comforts of family and home. I no longer had church fellowship or weekly sermons to fill my spirit. I fell out of relationship with

Blessed Passenger

God. I knew he was present and I certainly continued to pray, but I was definitely "in the world" trying to get myself together.

A typical weekend back home in Maryland, included heavy social drinking and partying with my friends. From the nightclubs of Baltimore to Washington DC, I was there. Often dressed in a sexy little outfit, accentuating all my best "assets" dancing to the latest club mix or go-go hit, competing for specific attention from the cutest guys in the building, and always shutting the club down. One morning, easily three or four AM, after ingesting several cocktails through the night, I was driving myself and three friends back to Columbia, MD from DC. A car accident in the road ahead on I-295 slowed the traffic, prolonging the typical forty-minute drunken journey even further. Two of my friends had already fallen asleep. As the car grew quiet and the sedating effects of alcohol took over, I too dozed off and began to drift off the road. My friend Melanie, the only person awake in the car, screamed my name from the back seat. I woke up to the sound of rumble strips under my tires and trees in front of me. It was a sobering moment — literally and figuratively. We made it home safely. I avoided vehicular manslaughter and DWI charges that night, but in a true moment of honesty, I must say I don't know how many alcohol-filled journeys I made it through. That night, or any other, could have easily derailed the entire trajectory of my life. But I lived to drink and drive again.

Casual drinking took on a new meaning as I became more focused on my career and met my second husband. At this time in my life, I was twenty-eight years old working on my license in professional counseling. We worked together as mental health counselors on a mobile crisis team for mental health and substance abuse populations in Baltimore City. How ironic, that my husband's drinking habits were a driving force for emotional and physical crisis in our family. He was a good man with a good heart—yet he had an unquenchable thirst for beer.

I was used to the happy-go-lucky party and have-a-good-time drunk. New to me was his brand of intoxication, which was angry, moody, and unpredictable. I grew weary of his belligerent episodes of disrespect and bladder incontinence, only for him to wake up the next morning as if it never happened. Watching someone you love act completely out of character is one of the hardest and most confusing things to experience. Alcohol slowly but surely drove a wedge in my marriage and seemed to dig up unresolved anger and frustration from my past. In my first marriage, I was sad and depressed with no voice to talk about the shame I was feeling; whereas in my second marriage, I was full of resentment and mad as hell. Yet and still, I was the common denominator.

My marriages were unhealthy and emotionally draining. I had more than enough reasons to blame these men for stealing my joy. I imagined no one would think otherwise of me if I ended up bitter, single, and resentful for the rest of my adult life. But at the end of the day, I chose these men. I married them. I had to face the fact that I had no idea what I was doing in marriage and if I truly desired the lifelong partnership my parents raised me in, then I had some soul-searching to do.

Now in my early to mid-thirties as the single mother of two daughters, dating and finding viable romances was a new task. I was working over forty hours a week in clinical management and finishing my doctorate in psychology. I no longer had the time, energy, or desire to frequent the latest hot spots in the city. My needs as a woman were changing and my responsibilities were immense. I found it difficult to meet a well-packaged man that was single, employed, good-looking, fun-loving, family oriented, and responsible. At times, I was trying to turn a well-packaged hoe into a husband. I quickly discovered it doesn't matter how good of a woman you think you are, a male hoe has no intention of honoring you with complete commitment or fidelity. I tried to convince myself that I was not looking for marriage, so just enjoy myself. But, we as women, are not built for casual sex. We are loving, emotionally driven beings with a built-in mothering instinct that gives us a central desire to nurture others. I was hopelessly single and defeated in relationships, often compromising my time for company. My friends and family were getting married around me and I was genuinely happy for them. Despite my trials and tribulations with marriage and relationships, I was nobody's hater. I was the eternal third or fifth wheel to my married friends and family. But I found contentment. I had a talk with God and figured... I guess it's time to get comfortable being single.

I shed years of built up anger and resentment by merely focusing on myself and trying to be a better mom. While I was working crazy hours trying to make ends meet, the girls were often in the care of my parents and other extended family. I was facing exhaustion and feared being an overworked therapist who spent too much time taking care of other people's children while neglecting her own. I was seeking balance over anything else — I didn't want to break my children. I didn't want to regret being emotionally or physically present for them. I didn't want to look back one day and say, "I should've been there." So, I began cutting back from work to be a "field trip" mom. I had long stints of singleness, not dating, not seeking...just chilling with my family and friends, some of whom were a little concerned...

Facebook Memory: May 4, 2013
Sonja > Melissa: Your Daily Horoscope
If you are single, it would be a sin against nature for you to spend the day holed up at home today. Get yourself out into the fresh air, rain, or shine, get out to see and be seen. Something is in the air today, and you could be lucky in more ways than one.

Blessed Passenger

Let me be clear, I never had a problem going out and meeting men. I'm a social butterfly, attractive, fun-loving; but it never resulted in anything longstanding or committed. At some point, my singleness became a choice over casual sex and dating games that did not get me past the temporary fix.

In trying to find my peace of mind, through the toxicity of domestic violence, separation/divorce, single motherhood, remarriage, alcoholism, a second separation-divorce, and being a dating single mom, I was often led back to me. I had to get honestly acquainted with the blind spots that were driving my decisions — emotionally, physically, spiritually, romantically, educationally, familial-ly — what was I trying to accomplish? Who was I trying to be? And how do I get there? What do I need to know about myself to make the best decisions for me and where I'm trying to go?

My soul searching and singleness drew me closer to God. It unearthed a whisper inside of me — an exhilarating force that you cannot grab with your hands. It is literally intangible, but powerful enough to drive me, and you, from blindness to blessings. *Blessed Passenger* is my testimony of being an unchurched woman, with a history of toxic relationships, misguided sexuality, and blind hope, who became drawn to *real talk*, bible-based Christian teaching and the essence of God. He has been the guiding force all along. He was with me far before I was with Him. Drawing close to Him allowed me relief amid the separation/divorce process; and comforted me through seasons of complicated grief. The intangible whisper of his voice has become more than familiar, and it lies at the foundation of all that I am today.

Despite seasons of grief, loss, relationship disappointment, and general discontent amidst some of life's most difficult situations, I am blessed. God has gifted me with wisdom, understanding, an emotional wholeness in His renewing spirit. He continues to keep his hands on me, nudge me, and guide me—and I trust him with my whole heart. It is by His grace that I don't look like what I have been brought through. I am blessed, walking in God's glory of deliverance and transformation.

1

Burnout: Life in the Balance

In February 2008, I began working at a residential treatment center (RTC) for adolescent girls. These young ladies were traumatized, aggressive, and oversexualized often struggling with depression and other mood disorders. They were deemed unsafe to attend public schools or live in the general community due to being a significant risk to themselves or others. I worked directly with some of the most clinically complicated adolescent cases in the State of Maryland and had previously been working in crisis care for about three years. This new job was not for the faint of heart. There was always a crisis. The collective experience of childhood trauma coupled with the inability to manage their emotions forecasted the continuous incidence of crisis. In a day's work, there were literally hundreds of emails sent between clinicians, treatment teams, residential staff, nursing, and administration to maintain the chain of communication required for the treatment process. The company provided Blackberry cell phones so that we were always an email or phone call away from a suicidal threat, a fight, an allegation, or safety issue that required near-immediate attention. The work was intense, and I had proven myself well-suited for it as I was promoted to a clinical management position in just under four months with the company.

Being in the middle of divorce from my second husband (artistically known as Janus), the promotion an approximate twenty-thousand dollar raise arrived just in time. Despite our previous agreement to maintain cost sharing of our two-bedroom condo until it was sold, Janus decided to relocate out of state. The residential market crash left the property slow to sell, which left me with an entire mortgage and all related housing expenses. Our two daughters, Imani-age nine from my first marriage, and Erin-age two, were not in position to raise themselves, so my "mommy hustle" was on an all-time high. I was finishing my doctorate in counseling psychology and writing my dissertation in the early hours of the morning while the girls were asleep. As the dawn broke, it was time to wake the kiddies and prepare for an unpredictable work day. Even though I was consistently sleep deprived and overworked, my professors marveled at my writing style and ability to articulate research material. I enjoyed my studies, but by the end of it all, I had a "let's get it done" mentality. Without steady child support or a co-parent in sight, I did not have time or energy to waste complaining about my situation. There was too much to do. I had to make ends meet and stay focused on providing for myself and my girls. My career and school work gave me something to focus on through the transition of single-parent struggles. I believed all the sleepless nights and following advancement would be pay off for my family in the end.

At work, the responsibility of crisis-oriented clinical management was crazy! It didn't take long for me to grow accustomed to the daily barrage of emails and end-of-shift notifications detailing the day's safety, security, and treatment issues. You had to be beyond committed to the work at hand, willing to sacrifice a lunch hour or consistent "punch out" on the clock because crisis does not have a clock. Crisis work does not typically fit into a neat nine-to-five window, so even though I was rushing from work to get to my daughter's basketball practice or driving somewhere with my family, I was often on my phone maintaining the loop of communication. I liked working at the RTC. The students, despite their tragic difficulties with abuse and neglect, were resilient and powerful, even in their weakest times. At work, I was privileged to witness and be a part of the change process that would impact their future lives in some way, hopefully positive. I also liked my coworkers—they were fun-loving, enjoyable people. We forged strong friendships through the stress of it all, and often leaned on each other for support and comic relief.

But I surely had moments when my mouth was unadulterated and unapologetic. If you caught me at the right space and time, the golden ticket was all yours. One time while sitting at a traffic light texting a friend, the car behind me beeped softly and I could see the driver motioning at me in the rear-view mirror. I was confused. As the car pulled into the neighboring lane, I looked over to see what the problem was. The elder gentleman driver began to roll down his window, so I thought he might have needed directions. As I rolled down my window, he proceeded to say, "You know it's illegal to do that now?" Without nearly a half-second's hesitation, I responded "What?! The light is red. You need to mind your d@mn business." For the first minute or two, I felt fully justified — it was illegal to talk on the phone and drive (not text), AND my car was sitting idle at a traffic stop! It wasn't until I proceeded a little further down the road, that I said, *"Good Lord, did I just cuss out an old man on the street?"* I was half-giggling, half-embarrassed of myself as I arrived home to tell my parents about it. All in all, that tempered short-fuse was just an example of my mind being pulled in ten directions. The juggling act of my mommy hustle was taking its toll. But by November 2009, the child support proceedings and final details of divorce were just coming into effect. It seemed like Janus was beginning to feel the wrath of the State of Maryland:

<u>Email from Janus: "Still Trying" November 18, 2009</u>

Hey M,

Just wanted to touch base with you since I know you're holding the fort down without any assistance. I've just sent some money through DSS (not much), but I'm trying. I will also be sending some money for Erin's Birthday and for the girls for Christmas. I will be sending that directly to you, so it doesn't get accounted for through DSS (that's o.k). According to DSS, I have to send all monies directly to them and they disperse to you. That sucks, but it is what it is. I certainly would have preferred to deal with you directly...things will get better. I am in the process of trying to obtain income to be able to increase the amount of funds that I will be sending and so it will be on a more regular basis. I've asked DSS to consider an adjustment (not to current arrears) to future support amount required because I just don't have enough to afford 1,000 a month. I'm sure you know that. I know that you have done all of this on your own and I am grateful and in debt to you for holding it down without assistance from me. I would like to be able to work something out with you that would be appropriate and attainable for future support. I have not forgotten my responsibilities and I am doing everything possible to meet obligations (things will get better). If at all possible, let me know what you think is possible in terms of coming up with a plan that is attainable and reasonable for you. Thanking you in advance.....J

P.S. Kiss my girls for me.

Dr. Melissa Tate-Scruse

Hey J,

Things are quite difficult for everyone financially. I have been holding it together best I can to support myself and the girls...not to mention extra, unaccounted for expenses with medical necessities and tax payments that we are BOTH responsible for. I'm not sure what your intention was when you picked up and moved but you changed the game dramatically in making decisions for yourself, which I believe were meant to spite me.... now it's coming back on you. (this is strictly my opinion)

At any rate, I would have preferred to work directly with you as well, but you took that decision out of both of our hands when you neglected to attend court. My going through the State was at the judge's direction due to not having received any money from you at all since you moved in August/September 2008. And to be honest, it's probably best to let a neutral party make the decisions so that things are not personalized.

I know that $1000+ is a lot of money, but again that is what the State came up with...not me. I need as much help as I can get in taking care of the kids. I work a lot of overtime to make ends meet and it does not come easy. I am tired and overworked...but I don't have a choice. So, to be quite frank, I don't have any sympathy for you at this time. Sympathy takes energy and I'm channeling my energy into taking care of these kids. I hope things work out for you financially because ultimately, it's the kids that suffer. Erin really likes going to school and I would like to keep her in it, but I may have to pull her out if things don't change soon. And that is not fair to her AT ALL!!!

So, my advice to you (take it or leave it) is do what you gotta do. I would appreciate help with Christmas and Erin's birthday. You know I'm not a chicken head parent, so it will be put to appropriate use. I don't think I'm in a position to make a decision about what is possible and attainable with regard to your income. My monthly expenses are high, as you well know. I still haven't sold the condo, so that's $1600 a month...school for Erin is $800 a month.... clothes, food, medical, entertainment.... need I say more.

Blessed Passenger

My frustrations were boiling, and it didn't seem like relief was coming fast enough. The burnout was setting in. After nearly two years at the RTC, I decided to use vacation time during the Thanksgiving Holiday. I was slated to be out of work for several days, from Wednesday until the following Monday. I cannot fully explain the amount of extra hustle it takes to prepare for an absence from crisis care—transferring clinical cases temporarily, notifying family and corresponding agencies of the vacation plan and liaison contacts, ensuring that all paperwork is complete and up-to-date, in addition to preparing your clinically traumatized clients (who often have abandonment issues) that you will be absent. It makes an already intense job, even more intense as you are pre-planning for what might occur in your absence. So, walking out of work on that Tuesday evening before Thanksgiving was exhilarating and much needed! I was hosting family dinner at my house for the first time. I spent Wednesday cleaning up and cooking, preparing for everyone to arrive. On Thursday, I had a full house of mom, dad, siblings, aunts, uncles and cousins of all ages. It was a typical holiday gathering for my family—enough food to feed a small village, family card games and board games, and football on the television. I went Black Friday shopping at midnight with my sister-cousin Staci, only to return home that Friday morning dreading a return to work on Monday. Everyone is prone to a little "Monday blues" but there I was *on a Friday*, already dreading work for Monday.

That was a very pivotal, unforgettable moment for me. I loved the field of psychology and still had a passion for mental health care, but I needed a change from that level of intensity. As a newly divorced, single mother of two daughters, I began to worry that I was going to sacrifice my relationships with them if I continued at that pace. My oldest daughter was approaching middle school at the time and had been in some little tit-for-tat *mean girl* drama at school. After being completely estranged from her biological father and losing her step-father to divorce, I had a recurring question bouncing around my mind: Am I spending too much energy taking care of other peoples neglected, traumatized children, only to perpetuate the issue in my own family?

I had not been in church fellowship in years, but it didn't stop me from praying. I had very brief, direct conversations with God: *Dear God, please don't let me break my children.* I began searching for other job opportunities outside of crisis care. With my doctorate in counseling psychology completed and the amount of experience I had in the field, I applied for a wealth of less-crisis oriented positions that would have aligned with my expertise—public schools, college professor, outpatient clinics—But nothing materialized. So, on top of being burned out, I was heavily frustrated that I was stuck in a job I no longer wanted.

In the following weeks, somehow my Blackberry became corrupted and I couldn't receive daily phone calls and emails on my work cell. Here was yet another hindrance to complicate my day. I felt out of the loop. I was one step behind, unable to stay on top of things as well as before. If a fight occurred in the middle of the night or if a child had a flashback episode that included self-injury behaviors, I didn't find out until I walked in the building. In the first few days, I felt unprepared for my 9am management meetings. During the day, the only way to check my email was from the desktop computer in my office. Without my Blackberry, I could not receive emails at the end of the shift or through the wee hours of the night and morning. After a few days, it still wasn't fixed, and I began to realize—perhaps my broken phone was a blessing in disguise.

Having the phone on my hip always kept me in crisis intervention mode. It kept me in anticipation of the next crisis—and there was always a crisis. It kept me on my toes, sharp, and ready to perform optimally at work; but what about at home? At home, I was distracted, often checking my work phone. I was physically present, but not always emotionally present or attentive to the moment. It was common for me to take an after-hours phone call or respond to emails as the need arose, which meant time and attention away from life outside of work—my life as a mother. Without my Blackberry for about a week, I was slowly deprogrammed from being in crisis intervention mode. Although it felt a little foreign from the way I had been operating for two years, it also gave me time to focus on other things. I was less distracted and less hurried. I realized I had not established the best boundaries between my work life and personal life.

That realization changed my whole perspective of how I had been setting myself up for stress. I had not fully allowed myself to be "off work." Once the phone was replaced, I decided to keep up those previously neglected phone boundaries. I stopped answering my phone and responding to emails after work. I decided that whatever crisis was waiting for me at 7pm, would be there for me at 7am when I was preparing for work the next morning. When I punched out at the end of the day, I was more intentional about enjoying my evenings with friends and family without checking my phone. This slight change made a difference in my evening and in the level of stress I allowed to impact me outside of work.

One Thursday evening in the following weeks of December, I left work to pick up my daughters and enjoy a middle school basketball game where my "friend" was coaching. We had been casually dating for a while (with a lot of sex and no true commitment) but we were steadily spending more time together. I was planning to take off work the next day to give myself a three-day weekend and take advantage of a little ME-time. As I was sitting in the gym and the game was concluding, I got a phone call from work. Keeping my *new* boundaries intact, I pushed the call to voicemail. The phone rang again. I pushed it to voicemail a second time. Within another minute, my phone rang a third time, which I answered with an attitude. *"Hello??"* It was Annette, the residential coordinator who managed one of the units I was responsible for.

"Tate, [*one of the girls*] tried to commit suicide. She's on the way to the hospital."

Colored with frustration, I said "Okaaay" as if to say, *why are you calling me with this?* Suicidal gestures, behaviors, and threats were common discussions in my line of work at the time. The population I worked with was very volatile and emotionally unstable. They often threw around phrases like "kill yourself" amongst one another, or "I might as well kill myself" when they did not get their way. We then proceed to put a plan in place to ensure safety and limit access to anything dangerous while we therapeutically support and process feelings to move beyond that emotional state. Our staff was equipped with medical personnel, doctors, nurses, mental health professionals, and behavior specialists to address this type of behavior on site. So, although conversations about suicide were common, it was not typical for a student to be rushed to the hospital—*yet I was still annoyed*.

Annette continued, "I just wanted to make sure you knew because the staff found her hanging and had to perform CPR 'til the ambulance arrived."

With a sigh, I said "Okay". I hung up the phone and sat there for a moment as the noise of an excited gymnasium was swirling around me. "I guess I'm going to have to go to work tomorrow." My friend saw my pause. "What's wrong?" he inquired.

"Nothing, I gotta go." The girls and I gathered our things, said our goodbyes, and walked to the car. On the way to the car, I called the job to see what was going on, but in my head, I was still annoyed that I had to head home prematurely. I couldn't even enjoy a basketball game and leisurely time with my friends. Regina, the clinical administrative specialist with a heart of gold, answered the phone, "Tate, this is not looking good. I don't think she's going to make it." The gravity of that phone call, of the dire situation, finally hit me. I was immediately overwhelmed with grief and confusion. As the details of what happened continued to unfold during that phone call on the drive home, I was saddened for the life that was teetering in the balance, and equally mad at myself for being so burnt out and desensitized to the magnitude of suicide. My thoughts were racing as I thought about that young lady in the hospital and wondered whether she would pull through. I thought about the staff and the other students I was responsible for, and I knew I had to go to work the next morning, even though I did not want to. I was filled with anger and sadness in my head, but I was numb in my expression of emotion. I cried myself to sleep that night and did not rest well at all.

As I arrived to work the next morning, everyone's grief and worst fears were collectively brought to the surface of discussion. We were in a shared state of shock, as we were debriefed about her critical condition, being managed on life support without brain activity, at the discretion of her family. I was tearful, but still stone-faced and irritable with the same running thought in my head: *I don't want to be here* [at work].

She laid in that hospital bed with the aftermath of her suicidal actions in full swing, as we, the treatment team, were tasked with telling nearly a hundred emotionally fragile girls the state of affairs. In my mind: *Ugh...I don't want to be here.* My boss informed us that a Crisis Counselor was contracted to be on site for the day to provide counseling and support as we needed. One of the therapists had already spoken with her and felt it was helpful. Being that the dying girl was one of my residents, everyone kept looking at me, checking on me, trying to support me. Again, in my mind, *I don't want to be here.* My supervisor then asked me directly, if I wanted to talk to the crisis counselor, to which I declined. As the meeting room cleared, everyone retreated to their own sanctuary of comfort. I just sat there, *irritated*, and talked with my best friend Sonja, who was also a clinical manager. She asked, "How are you feeling? Are you sure you don't want to go talk to her?"

"Unless she is here to offer me a new job, I don't need to talk to her." It was such a quick, unemotional statement of my mind, and I'm sure it sounded very abrupt and cold. My supervisor returned to the meeting room within a couple of minutes. She politely impressed upon me that my talking with the crisis counselor was not really an option. As I walked up the hallway toward the meeting space, I thought: *Let's just get this over with.* I entered the room to find a very poised and polished African American woman who introduced herself as Dr. Renee Harding.

The session began with a typical introduction of who I was and my role in the company. She asked my connection to [the girl]. I took the next ten or fifteen minutes to vent very transparently and share how I was feeling—About how I was feeling burned out and pondering my position at the company in the first place; how this impending death was derailing my intention to take the day off; how I don't have any feelings of blame toward anyone for this situation because my staff is great and dealing with their own feelings of self-blame and guilt; how suicidal people are typically decided about their suicide and leave survivors with little room to have changed the outcome; and about my personal belief that knowing this girl and her inward thoughts and feelings has left me feeling like this may have been an "oops" that went past the point of her control. I also shared that I was angry that she is now stuck on life support with no brain activity. I expressed my belief that this was between [her] and God, and that we did what we could do to save her, but it's not our call. I was open, honest, and appropriately tearful, as I took full advantage of this woman's ear. But I noticed an odd *shift* in our counseling session. Whereas our discussion seemed to begin as her supporting me, inquiring about my grief, and allowing me to share my feelings; somehow it shifted to more focused inquiry of me, my credentials, and my professional experience — kind of like *a job interview.*

Dr. Harding sat for a moment looking at her notes. She coyly stated, "This is a little unorthodox, but I do not believe that things happen by chance. I have a job for you." I sat up straight in utter disbelief as what I had previously spoken before walking into the office had come to pass. After months of feeling burnt out and job searching with no results, this tragedy was unfolding something right in front of me! She continued to say, "I believe that you're probably doing an excellent job here, but I don't feel like this is the final destination in your career. I think this is serving as a highway to something more for you, and although your experiences here, including this death, have been pivotal in your professional growth I don't see that your talents should remain here." I was astounded. As much as I did not want to be in that building or talk with that woman, that counseling session lit a fire inside of me. It was the fire I needed in that moment for all the grief, anger, and confusion I was feeling; and it continues to serve as a memorable moment in shifting my career direction. Dr. Harding proceeded to share her contact information with me and discuss a part-time position working at her outpatient agency. She was in search of a clinical supervisor and therapist and encouraged me to call her whenever I was available. Wow, talk about speaking something into existence. Despite the grief that continued to weigh heavy on my heart that day, and perpetually resonated amongst many of us at the RTC for months thereafter, I needed that glimpse of hope.

Through the sadness, I went on a frantic job-seeking rampage. Dr. Harding's offer was exciting, but I was in no position to leave my full-time salaried employment for a twenty-hour/week part-time job without benefits. There was no way I could provide for my family like that. I searched and applied for positions all over town at various universities, outpatient mental health clinics, local school boards, and surrounding hospitals, to minimal response. It felt like a sick joke. Clearly, I could sit in front of a working professional and present quite well, even amidst a state of crisis. But I couldn't even get a job interview or a call back. I sat stagnant in the same position for another eight months, all the while prayerful. The Director of the RTC created a position specifically with me in mind, which allowed me to transition to a lateral position with more flexibility. *Facebook Memory: "Prayer is mine...He's listening.* It relieved some of my frustrations of feeling unbalanced between work and home because I was able to leave work in the afternoons just as my children were getting out of school. But crisis care is crisis care, nonetheless. The mommy hustle must go on.

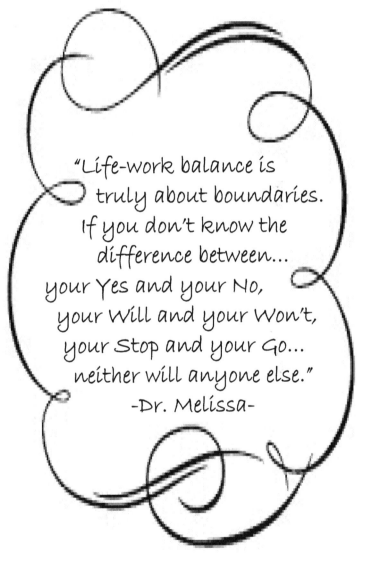

"Life-work balance is
truly about boundaries.
If you don't know the
difference between...
your Yes and your No,
your Will and your Won't,
your Stop and your Go...
neither will anyone else."
-Dr. Melissa-

Dr. Melissa Tate-Scruse

2

Relief & Grief

Even though the divorce was final, Janus and I continued to have our communication difficulties. He seemed to call me from time to time with a mixed sense of entitlement and self-pity. In one breath, he would say things like *"Your last name is still Tate. You'll always be my wife."* In another breath, he had a sob story of why he couldn't do more financially, quick to refer to *"Dr. Tate and all the money in the bank"* because I earned my doctoral degree and was working in management. It did not make sense to indulge him in conversation. I laughed at how silly and intoxicated he sounded — despite his denial that he had not been drinking. I was relieved to be legally divorced and separated from the burden of carrying his mess; but he had not been to visit the children since he moved.   Imani, now almost eleven years old, was beginning to question his absence: *Why did daddy move away? Was it my fault? Did he ever love me? What about my real dad, did he love me?* It pissed me off to see her stuck in feelings of grief, loss, and self-blame. The same boundary of separation and divorce that gave me a sense of relief was now the source of her grief. My relief — Her grief.

I took a deep breath as I pondered how I was supposed to answer her questions without letting my resentment toward him smack her in the face. It's one thing for Dr. Tate to counsel someone else's child through abandonment issues, but this child was mine. "It's not your fault. Daddy and I do not get along and it wasn't healthy for us to stay together. I'm sorry he decided to move away, and I'm not 100 percent sure why. But I know he loves you and your sister very much. I have not spoken to your real dad in years. I don't know where he is or what he is doing. I'm sorry they are not here to answer your questions. I don't have all the answers. Just know that I'm here and I'm not going anywhere." I let her cry, wiped her tears, and consoled her as long as she needed. I reminded her that she is surrounded by love even though her fathers are not here, and I encouraged her to cherish the relationships we had. Later that evening, I was still heated. My mind was racing with agitation. I took my feelings to him the best way I knew how.

Email: June 5, 2010 | Re: Disappointed

Dear J,

I'm pretty sure our last conversation didn't go the way you anticipated. I don't feel that you recognize the difficulty I'm in caring for the kids and trying to keep a roof over our head and food in our mouths. The "Dr" title that you are so quick to bring up does not bring the financial clout that you think it does. I'm not in a position to work the overtime hours anymore at work, so my money has been cut significantly.

I need your help. The $100 every other month you send is really a slap in the face. That only contributes toward 1 week of Erin's half day tuition for school. What about the other 51 weeks a year??? She's only going from 9am-12pm because that's all that I can afford...and that is now in jeopardy since my money has been cut. She's getting to the point where she needs to be going for a full day. But I can't afford that by myself. Never mind clothes, shoes, food, medical, etc....that sh*t don't fall from the sky because I dream it. I don't see that you're making an effort to do all that you can to support your children. As it was in our marriage, your desires continue to take precedent.

I lost faith in you as a Husband a long time ago. I've now lost faith in you as a Father because of your absent neglectful ways. And because of that, I've lost faith in you as a Man. I've tried not to harbor negative feelings about you, but you don't make it easy. I have yet to mention the emotional impact all of this has on the kids...that Erin likes to call my father "Daddy" even though she knows he's her grandfather. I Thank God she recognizes in him what a Father is supposed to be. Imani feels you don't love her and is wondering whether you ever loved her. She has now added you to the same list as her biological father, who she has no memories of. Doesn't that say a lot about your relationship with her during our marriage and since our divorce? I'm left to do the psychological damage control on your broken promises to her...and your occasional $100 and wack @ss, empty greeting cards don't address these things. But despite all of this mess, I'm raising two beautiful, smart, resilient, extremely loved girls. And that's why I'm called a Mother, a title you will never fully respect the way that it deserves. Your absence in this respect is probably best because you are so emotionally damaged and self-medicated [with alcohol]. I won't allow you to cast your mess on to my kids.

I'm not really sure what I'm trying to accomplish in sending this email. I guess I feel the need to put it on the record that I'm so truly disappointed in you because I thought you to be a better person than this. But apparently, your true colors are in full bloom. I am going to let go of my feelings so that I can be at peace. I am letting go...and letting God take this burden of you from me and my children. The government and the courts will decide your fate in due time. And God will be your ultimate judge.

In the meantime, don't call me anymore with that egotistical, self-registered, pity party...I do not have the time, energy, or patience for your foolery. I am not your friend or enabler. Take it elsewhere. Peace be unto you.... Melissa

P.S. I've included your parents in this email because I'm sure you have them thinking you are doing more than you are. I'm not keeping anymore of your dirty little secrets because its toxic. And it's beyond time to it let go. One day you will recognize that.

I didn't want to be bitter, angry, or spiteful, but I probably was. I just wanted him to man up and be responsible. I was too blind to realize that "responsible" is not who I married. I married a responsible-*looking* man with a broken spirit and a terrible drinking habit. He knew how to put on a responsible costume, but he also knew how to take it off. The toxic fallout of his drunken behaviors and inconsistencies wore me out, and I grew into a resentful, rather angry, sexless wife. I prayed for God to lift the anger from my spirit and bring me peace of mind.

I retreated to music as a sanctuary. The right song in the right moment accentuated my mood with an exclamation point! The perfect culmination of mood, music, and melody was like food to my soul. I could get lost for hours in a broad range of eclectic sounds from classics to contemporary — Billie Holiday, Esperanza Spalding, India Arie, Stevie Wonder, you name it. I also started listening to contemporary gospel music around that time. I vividly recall passing my dissertation defense after almost four years of graduate studies, late nights, and early mornings through marriage, pregnancy, job changes, separation and divorce, I played Marvin Sapp's *Never Would've Made It* on the repeat cycle all the way home. Thinking about all the built-up stress over the years and the dark, angry, depressed places I had been in previous years, I cried my face off the entire 45-minute drive from Washington DC. I was in awe of what I had just completed yet fully aware that I did not do it by myself.

Divorce is arguably one of the most stressful life transitions one can experience. Going through it for a second time, now with two daughters to support, forced me to come to terms with all the changes that were happening around me. Although legally relieved from the toxicity of an unhealthy marriage, I was now in the phase of shifting my mindset and rebuilding my life. It is therapeutically appropriate to consider separation, divorce, and relational breakups a grief and loss process. There were losses and symbolic "deaths" occurring in nearly every area of my life. Let's put it into perspective:

Relationship Status

My identity as a wife died, for a second time. Some people spend a lifetime playing the "blame game" remaining stuck in the debris of a broken relationship. Although I had more than enough reasons to blame my ex-husbands for the demise of our nuptials, I was the common denominator. You know the old saying, first time shame on you, second time…shame on me. That's where I was—I had shame on me. At that time, I was the product of a 40+ year marriage of middle school sweethearts, and I heavily believed in the sanctity and foundation of marriage. But I was, evidently, doing something wrong. I was the blind passenger on an emotional rollercoaster of my loved ones' toxic behaviors—alcoholism, mood swings, aggression, jealousy, possession, insecurity, and loneliness. These relationships did not match my mindset for a fruitful marriage, family, or lifestyle, and I, like so many people, did not allow myself to realize this until I was already married. I was impatient and blind, sweeping things under the rug. Blinded by love. Blinded by the desire to have a family. Blinded by shame. And blinded by trust. In the aftermath of separation and divorce, you begin to wonder if you could love, trust, and marry again. I was embarrassed to be divorced a second time. I grieved my marital status, uncertain whether I would be a wife again.

My "wifey status" died, leaving me single and intrinsically craving a viable relationship to share love. Or perhaps I was looking for someone to affirm that another separation and divorce wasn't my fault. I believed I was a good woman and would be a good wife to the right man. But my "picker" was broken. As my first ex-husband's father once told me, "You can do bad by yourself. My son has good intentions, but good intentions can pave the way to hell." I was dating and marrying men with no emotional availability to give me the sense of lifelong security I required as a wife. In the aftermath of divorce, I wasn't dating the right men—often engaging in sexual relationships without ideal commitment, or a sense of security. The men I was choosing had flawed ideas of relationships, so how were they going to be good boyfriends, let alone husbands?

Parenting Status

The new marital status also changes the parenting status. I went from a two-parent home with the expectation of partnership in childcare and household responsibilities, to single parenthood with a pending ex-husband who decided to relocate from the area. He was minimally involved in taking care of and visiting the children during the separation process when he resided five miles away, but at least he lived around the corner. His decision to move out of state changed the game dramatically. He relieved himself of the expectation or option to be considered for physical support and assistance. I was officially a single parent, to which I enlisted the help of family to surrogate my childcare needs. I was fortunate to have the familial support, for I recognized everyone does not have a reliable support network to assist in that transition. Unfortunately, some may elect to remain in an unhealthy situation to alleviate that burden.

In other situations where both parties remain committed to be an involved parent, separation and divorce brings the expectation of co-parenting with someone you have a history of difficulties with. You have struggled to partner with them in marriage, yet it is time to mesh parenting decisions? This indeed has its share of challenges as the children often feel torn between the parents even in the best of co-parenting situations. It requires you to separate your spousal judgement from the parenting role—meaning even though your ex struggled to meet your needs and desires as a spouse, does he/she have the initiative to keep your children safe, cared for, and provided for? If the answer is yes, you do not have the right to exert your spousal agitation onto the children, using them as a pawn to manipulate or irritate your ex. Period.

In other cases, people get separated and divorced premature of having children. They are forced to ponder their life circumstance and possibilities of their biological clock allowing them to find a new love and have children of their own. I encourage people to be mindful of the urge to rush into another relationship, or stay settled in an unhealthy relationship, for fear that they may not be able to have children in the future. It is also typical for people to stay in an unhealthy marriage "for the kids" — worried about single parenthood, co-parenting, or trying to date/remarry while you have children. "Baby Mama/Daddy" drama is a legitimate concern as parenting status changes.

Financial Status

Finances are a primary factor of family stability. Separation and divorce can unravel that sense of stability as each party then becomes financially responsible for their own household. In my situation, I managed the stress of financial cares by diving into work and school. I felt a frenzied energy to take care of my family, despite a loss of husband and income, which led me to be overworked and burned out. I worked overtime, taking on a larger caseload in an already crisis-oriented job, which was exhausting. I eventually moved in with my parents, who were able to support me through the long hours and responsibilities, while providing a sense of stability for the girls. You may find that it's time to downsize to a smaller, more affordable situation because the person who once "had your back" is no longer there.

Emotional status

Amidst the separation and divorce process, people will find themselves raw with emotions. From sadness to anger to loneliness, it is common to feel out of sorts through the transition. In my case, the emotional fallout of separation and divorce was heightened by the toxicity of verbal abuse, physical dispute, and humiliating substance abusing behaviors that chipped away at my personal integrity.

My emotional health was unsteady as I tried to consider the greater needs of marriage and family — often bottling up feelings of confusion, sadness, anxiety, frustration, and shame. I was ashamed of the broken state were going through for fear of judgement. And I didn't want to hear the *I told you so's* or *why are you still with him's* intentions because I was married — a decision I made with long-term intentions. I did not agree to either marriage with divorce in mind, so I had a great deal of confusion and self-doubt surrounding my marital choices and how I ended up in — not just one, but — two broken marriages in less than 10 years. You know the old saying: *First time, shame on you.* Second time, shame on me. That's exactly what I had — I had shame on me.

Definition of Shame

1. painful feeling of humiliation or distress caused by the consequences of wrong or foolish behavior.
2. A loss of respect or esteem; dishonor
3. A regrettable or unfortunate situation or action

Synonyms: humiliation, guilt, embarrassment, discomfort, remorse, disgrace, dishonor, indignity, misfortune, stigma

Antonyms: Pride, glory, honor

I was battling the shame and distress of how I got myself in these unfortunate marital situations. *Regret.* I was carrying the cumulative memories of shameful, embarrassing experiences I had throughout those marriages. *Humiliation.* With each passing marital trauma, I became increasingly aware that I was losing respect for myself, as I was repeatedly compromising ME and everything I knew myself to be for relationships that were not making me a better person. *Loss of respect or esteem.* I felt saddened and crazy as my peace of mind was suffering. *Grief.* I was fighting for my personal integrity as much as I was battling the toxicity of those relationships. *Indignity.* At the end of the day, if you are covered with various degrees of guilt and shame, unable

Blessed Passenger

to take *pride* in yourself and who you are, how can you be a good wife or mother?

That was the echoing question in my head, as I was often consumed with worry about the example I was showing my daughters. I wondered how the family drama would impact their growing minds. If I felt thwarted and sheltered in my marriage, how would they feel growing up in our home? How would remaining in an abusive or toxic marriage impact *their* self-esteem and eventual marital choices?

> *A healthy individual identity is the foundation of healthy relationships. If either party has an unstable, immature, unhealthy, broken, toxic, codependent, traumatized Individual Identity, the relationship will reflect it.*
>
> *-Dr. Melissa*

The ultimate decision to separate from marriage was hinged on two things:

1. My intrinsic need for self-respect; and
2. The desire to be a healthy mother for my children.

Leaving abuse, toxicity, and unhealthy family interactions was the first step to restoring ME. The shame of divorce was eventually outweighed by the need to rebuild the individual ME, feel whole, and be proud of who I was. Pride and shame cannot occupy the same space at the same time. I needed to be able to look myself in the mirror, knowing I made a healthy decision for my well-being and for the good of my children. If I could stand on that declaration, there was no more space for shame.

From the outside looking in, I seemed happy, working hard to glue all the broken pieces together the best I could. Enjoying time with my family and friends was easy. Going to work, driving my success – no problems there either. I was good at compartmentalizing my feelings, putting them in a box to focus on more pressing tasks—like taking care of my children, or diving into work or school.

The difficulties came in dating and believing that I was destined for marriage. There was a quiet vulnerability under the mask of strength, independence, and lighthearted fun. My family-oriented desires for true, sincere relationship went unmet, and I was faced with bouts of loneliness. In the grief process of separation, divorce, and other breakups, people tend to seek replacement relationships to fill the void. Dating with a broken heart in the aftermath of divorce led me to settle for an oversexualized "fun affair"

> *Sometimes the best cure for loneliness is to spend so much time alone –in singleness with yourself, at one with your thoughts, dependent on no one or nothing, developing self-acceptance and personal esteem — that you no longer feel lonely.*
>
> *-Dr. Melissa -*

with a man that was not ready for commitment. Be careful not to cast your past hurts and untethered desires onto the next person, or you will perpetually make the same mistakes with a different partner. Sometimes the best cure for loneliness is to spend so much time alone — in singleness with yourself, unified with your thoughts, dependent on no one or nothing, developing self-acceptance and personal esteem — that you no longer feel lonely.

Spiritual Status

Although I had been disconnected from talking with God regularly for several years, spending time alone in my thoughts caused me to think existentially. I wanted to find the PEACE of my mind. No more shame, depressed thoughts, anger, or resentment — I didn't like the way it felt. I had to get an honest acquaintance with the blind spots that were driving my thoughts and decisions — emotionally, physically, spiritually, romantically, educationally, familial-ly — what was I trying to accomplish? Who was I trying to be? And how do I get there? What do I need to know about myself to make the best decisions for me and where exactly am I trying to go?

Whether you believe in God or not, when trying to provoke change in your mind and spirit, you have to believe in something. What you believe precedes your thoughts, feelings, and behaviors. One of my strongest declarations was that I didn't want to be another bitter, angry black woman. I believed I was supposed to be a wife and mother, a family woman; but if I wasn't content and solidified in who I was as a woman, I would never achieve the viable loving romantic relationship I desired. I started with me. Staying focused on me and the things I had the power to change in my life allowed me to get in touch with my instincts—that internal voice that tells you yes from no, right from wrong, and good from bad. From time to time, my instincts rose up with such authority and compelled me to make profound life decisions. I couldn't ignore what was developing inside of me.

Identity Crisis

As my adult life began to unfold, I saw pieces of me in jaw-dropping movie scenes, like *What's Love Got To Do With It?* And *Why Do Fools Fall In Love?* —except I was the leading lady. My first marriage was unhealthy at day one. The spirits of anger, envy, narcissism, and fears of abandonment were heavy in my first husband and therefore played out in our marriage. There I was, a new wife and mother at the age of twenty-two—depressed, emotionally abused, and naïve to the ingredients of a good marriage. It wore on my spirit and chipped away at the woman I thought I was. In my second marriage seven years later, I married a good-natured man with a terrible habit. The lovable person I knew him to be was easily condemned to irresponsible foolishness after a few beers. His drinking-and-driving was dangerous, and the drunken behaviors became an emotionally taxing burden. It watered a seed of anger and resentment that drove a wedge between us. I found myself lonely, angry, and resentful on the heels of another failed marriage, yet I was the common denominator. Although I was fully equipped with enough ammunition to blame these men for my state of being, I had some serious soul searching to do. My identity was in crisis.

Something in my spirit told me I was designed for better, but I had a decision to make. I had to decide whether to walk in bitterness and blame OR be the "me" I was destined to be. I was not going to be able to do both. My spirit was in jeopardy as long as a I held onto blame and resentment, so I had to be very decisive about regaining my peace of mind as to no longer allow depression, shame, anger or embarrassment to infiltrate my being. I didn't like myself in those emotional places, nor did I trust my anger, so I was on a mission to be a person I liked. Separation and divorce legally released me from the responsibility of riding that emotional roller coaster and allowed me to realign myself and my life with the actual identity I once had in my mind. As I walked away from toxic relationships and channeled my grief toward being someone I liked and could be proud of, a sense of relief came over me.

YES, RELIEF—defined as alleviation, ease or deliverance through the removal of pain, distress, or oppression. That's it. I was delivered from emotional pain and marital oppression, and I was gifted relief. Relief allowed me to exhale deep, no longer holding my breath in nervous anticipation or anger or frustration. Relief allowed me to regain my composure and redefine my direction. Relief gave me focus. I was relieved and delivered and able to refocus.

How do you spell RELIEF?

*R*EALITY
Accept the reality of your situation. You are trying to focus on the fairy tale, idea, or thought that is in your mind when all the evidence around you says it's a lie. I remember working so hard to convince my second husband that his drinking was tearing our family apart. After a long night of inexcusable drunken behavior, I had an idea I believed would shock him and bring him back to reality. I taped a picture of our family to the bathroom mirror and I wrote in bold, red lipstick "You're killing us!" As I was writing, I locked eyes with myself in the mirror. There was such an intense look of pain and desperation on my face. It stopped me dead in my tracks. I was working so hard to sustain the idea of family I had in my mind, while everything around me called that devil a lie. The fact

remained that if he decided to keep on drinking there was absolutely nothing I could do to stop him. I could write on every mirror in America. I could pour out all the beer in the house. I could refuse to have sex with him. I could pray until I was breathless. But at the end of the day, the decision to drink was his and his alone. The reality and helplessness in that situation was heavy truth, but it allowed me to give up the power struggle. When you're in a toxic relationship, the truth hurts and something about the lie feels better. So, we spend all this emotional and physical energy trying to avoid the truth of the matter. Proverbs 23:23 NLT says, *"Get the truth and never sell it; also get wisdom, discipline, and good judgement."* Without truth, you will continue to lack wisdom and understanding, therefore unable to exercise good judgement or have good relationships. So, what is the truth? What is the REALITY of your situation? What are you failing to see, acknowledge, and let go?

Here is something else to consider: Beliefs are not always truth. If it were so, our beliefs would be called FACTS. Sometimes our beliefs corroborate the foundation of emotional lies that keep us stuck. For example, I believe marriage is a commitment that should not be broken. My parents have been married for almost 50 years and I once believed I would be as well. Once I was in an abusive, emotionally toxic marriage, I found myself in conflict with the pre-marital beliefs that were in my head. I was in anguish. I felt like a failure. My marriage was in shambles, seemingly beyond repair, and in that situation, my beliefs needed to be confronted. I had to relieve myself of the shame and embarrassment of potential divorce because it was holding me emotionally hostage in an abusive marriage. What beliefs do you need to confront about your broken relationships?

*E*MOTIONAL COMPOSURE

Toxic relationships are most easily described as an emotional rollercoaster. They have the capacity to bring you to the brink of happiness and the brink of disaster in a moment's time. It constantly challenges your breaking point and tolerance for "craziness", and your emotional response can often become a part of the bigger problem.

During my ex-husband's drunken tirades, he became belligerent and profane, as if he was looking for an argument. My attempts to ignore him or excuse the behavior as "liquor talk" once escalated to me slapping him across the face when his words got too slick. The identified *drinking problem* is now further complicated by my *anger management* problem. Consider this…What if he would have hit me back? In a toxic relationship, the emotional rollercoaster has so many "what ifs"; and the potential for emotional and/or physical damage becomes more dangerous with time. If feeling sad, uneasy, anxious, confused, desperate, defensive, or perhaps aggressive, becomes your "new normal", you have officially lost your peace of mind. It's time to regain your emotional composure.

Blessed Passenger

Composure is synonymous with being poised, settled, and focused. Without composure, you are subject to a wrath of emotions and behaviors that contribute to the unhealthiness of the relationship. Emotional composure gives you stronger discernment and allows you to make better decisions in the face of toxic behaviors. When your mindset is emotionally composed and settled, you are more capable of recognizing Mr. or Mrs. Wrong for who they are.

Emotional composure allows you to regain the "you" that makes you feel like "you". What was going on in your life the last time you felt emotionally composed and settled in your thoughts? Reacquaint yourself with the frame of mind, activities, and people that were in your life at that time, if possible. The relationships and activities that are not in alignment with the more composed version of you, are likely not in your best interest. Romans 16:17 ESV --"*I appeal to you, brothers, to watch out for those who cause divisions and create obstacles contrary to the doctrine that you have been taught; avoid them.*" If you truly desire a sense of relief, some people in your life have got to go! Take a moment and think about the last three situations in your life that you did something out of character. Who was there? Who cosigned on your mess? Who did you allow to set the stage for your demise? Re-evaluate your team around the emotionally composed you.

It is also quite possible that you have never had the character of composure. In these cases, people are often a product of their environment—perhaps raised in messy family situations—in which case you have been raised and groomed to accept mess. It is an unfortunate truth that your journey for discovering emotional composure may require both physical and emotional distance from your family.

*L*ONELINESS VS. ALONENESS

In the aftermath of toxic, messy relationships, life may be feeling a little more hopeful and breathable. The stress of the emotional rollercoaster is draining, so you may find new energy in having released the burden of arguing, or worrying, or fighting with someone week after week. Having less burdens and stress, makes you appear more attractive, so it is inevitable that you may consider dating or someone may express romantic interest in you. Flirting with a new prospect is exciting and fun. It obviously feels good to be wanted. But please be careful. By far, the worst relationship advice I have ever heard: "The best way to get over one man/woman is to get under another." If any of your friends and loved ones encourage that, you should consider another source of advice.

Being alone and getting reacquainting with yourself is the best thing you can do. When you have been in a toxic relationship it is common to suppress parts of yourself for the sake of the relationship. Your "individual identity" can become weakened by your "relationship identity" because you had to spend so much energy to keep the peace with your boo. In that case, you've sacrificed things you like for things he likes…or you've stopped hanging out with friends/family because of his jealousy…or perhaps you've been holding in so many secrets about your relationship to avoid judgement. In either situation, your individual identity needs some attention after a break up. That could include going to therapy, picking up a retired hobby, or reuniting with good friends/family you've been estranged from. It should also include getting comfortable with being alone. And because you were used to the high-energy of an emotional rollercoaster relationship, being alone will sometimes feel lonely.

Loneliness is a state of being alone that includes sadness or anxiety. With loneliness there is a profound craving for connection to someone, often a romantic partner. It is a common phase in the grieving process after a loss, break-up, or death of a loved one. Even in the healthiest of breakups, you should be prepared to manage feelings of loneliness as not to jump into another unhealthy situation. This is when it gets real. This is the time when a phone call or text from the ex, or some other miscellaneous character, seems comforting. This is the moment when you will start to wonder if the relationship was really *that bad*. You may have old pictures or text messages or memorabilia of some kind. Box it up. Throw it away. Delete. You will want to rush through feelings of loneliness just to consider having company. In these spaces, you will be prone to entertain the wrong kind of company, and perhaps mistake a temporary lack of loneliness for new love.

In 2009 after my second divorce, I was casually dating a man that was several years younger than me. He was fun to hang around, always made me laugh, and reminded me to enjoy life around me. Despite all the key ingredients of a committed relationship, i.e. L words, date nights, sex, sleepovers, meeting the parents/friends/kids, etc., he was still in playboy mode and did not have the capacity to fully commit to me. At the time, I didn't consider myself lonely, but I surely became dependent on his company. I craved a commitment from someone that was non-committal. I compromised my standards for company. I mistook a lack of loneliness for love.

Here's my advice: *Get used to being alone.* Go to a movie or take a walk by yourself; and do so regularly. Get used to coming home to an empty bed and get re-accustomed to sleeping alone. *How long will this take?* You should spend enough time alone that it no longer feels lonely. Spending time alone should not feel like a task or a burden—It should feel like an opportunity. It's an opportunity to design your day based on your needs, not those of the relationship. Revisit some goals you've been unable to complete because of the relationship drama. There is always room for personal improvement when you are alone, but loneliness distracts you from the work. How can you best use your alone time?

*I*NVEST IN YOU

Investment is the act of devoting time, effort, or energy to something with the expectation of a worthwhile result. You likely devoted a lot of time, effort, and energy to keeping a toxic, dead-end relationship alive. You lived each day in anxiety and anticipation of how to keep things peaceful and minimize dispute. That could include wearing your clothes a certain way, minimizing conversation with others, being home when he/she wants you to be home, preparing things the way she likes, or perhaps buying personal gifts or surprises to brighten their day. The *Relationship Identity* (all the needs, wants, and desires of the relationship) has eclipsed your *Individual Identity* (all your personal needs, wants, and desires). When you are so focused on trying to make a toxic, emotionally bankrupt person happy, it is inevitable to lose sight of yourself and what makes you happy. Hear me now: The investment, time, effort, and energy you spend trying to cultivate someone else's happiness is futile. Happiness comes from within. If that emotional bank is empty, your time, efforts, and energy will never pay off. It is equivalent to trying to fill up a holey bucket—it will continue to leak. And perhaps you invested several months and years to figure there will not be a worthwhile result.

Once the break up or separation occurs, *give yourself* all the time, effort and energy that you would have invested in the toxic relationship. That time does not have to feel lonely or idle. More than likely, you neglected other friends, loved ones, school work, hobbies, or activities to invest in making the relationship look pretty. Take a step back and re-invest your time, efforts, and energy into worthwhile relationships. Invest in activities and people who make you feel worthy, who make you laugh, who support you, or those who increase your knowledge. Invest in things and people who build you up instead of tear you down. Make a list of five people who have had your back over the years — the ones who have been your cheerleaders, your confidantes, your prayer warriors, who have celebrated you, and have rarely been the source of your confusion. Re-invest in those relationships because you have likely been distant from them, or strained them, as you chose the toxic partner over them. Don't be ashamed of that — own it and do better. Figure out a way to celebrate them for being loyal to you when you were struggling to be loyal to yourself.

Furthermore, you need to re-invest in your spirit. Being in a toxic, emotionally draining relationship with someone, leaves your inner strength and sense of peace disrupted. Your inner-man, your spirit, your sense of self — separate from all those around you — needs attention too. In the aftermath of divorce and other miscellaneous breakups over the years, I prayed fervently for God to restore my peace of mind. I just wanted the confusion, heartache, and resentment to hush. I prayed: *"God, relieve me of anger, bitterness, and resentment. Don't let it rest in my spirit or come from my mouth. Restore me to who you designed me to be. Instead, allow peace in my mind and heart, make me whole, so that when the right man comes along,*

I'm prepared to love him as he deserves." I recited some version of this prayer to myself regularly. Long before I was firmly planted in my relationship with Christ, this was a personal meditation and mantra during quiet moments when I needed to get myself in check. Spiritual investment requires quiet time, personal moments, purposeful reflection, and a willingness to look inward with the ultimate goal being a new settled energy, attitude, and mood. With a settled energy and spirit, your actions and ability to make healthier decisions soon follows.

*E*DUCATION
Information and knowledge is power. In the aftermath of a divorce or in breaking off a toxic relationship, you may need to increase your understanding of the various situations that were a part of the relationship. This could include gaining an understanding of several types of abuse, alcoholism, addiction, codependency, enabling behaviors, intimate partner violence, toxic family dynamics, physical health issues, and/or mental illness. Seek counseling, attend a support group, talk to a doctor/physician, or relevant professional. Hosea 4:6 says *"My people are destroyed for lack of knowledge"*. Do not allow the shame of your personal situation to keep you stuck in an uninformed state of mind, thus likely to repeat poor, unhealthy choices.

FUTURE

Where are you headed? Do you have a goal in mind, and are your actions in accordance with that goal? James 1:8 says *"a double-minded man is unstable in all his ways."* It is impossible to walk in your true destiny and find your healthiest relationships if you're still grieving and surrounding yourself with the toxic ones. After shedding yourself of unhealthy relationships, it is easy to get stuck in dwelling on your current situation. Shift your thoughts to define your personal ideas, thoughts, and goals. Define your future.

❖ What do I want out of life?

_____

_____

_____

❖ What do I enjoy doing?

_____

_____

_____

❖ What talents and skills do I have? What am I good at doing?

_____

_____

_____

❖ What gets me motivated?

_____

_____

_____

❖ Who do I admire and why?

_____

_____

_____

❖ Who do I want to be in 1 year? 5 years? 10 years?

      o 1:_____

_____

_____

      o 5:_____

_____

_____

      o 10:_____

_____

_____

A Child's Grief from Separation-Divorce

As I was basking in new found RELIEF, freedom and independence, my oldest daughter, Imani, was pushing through a bevy of feelings about separation, divorce, and family changes that were outside of her control. I had more than enough reasons to justify my divorce, but she wasn't necessarily aware of those reasons. All she knew was we were moving out and the man she previously called "daddy" was moving away from our Maryland home. To add insult to injury, his moving date fell on her birthday.

The fatherly presence that brought her mother to marriage, also brought her a little sister and younger step-brother. The family she had grown accustomed to was now permanently altered by separation, divorce, and relocation. The absence of a biological father in her life meant a second paternal absence for her to work through. She was no longer able to see her step-brother on a weekly basis. And single parenthood meant we had to move in with my parents to make ends meet. MY relief in separation and divorce paved the way for her earliest experiences with grief.

Defining Grief

Although grief is formally described as a deep sorrow associated with death; grief also transcends death to include reactions to loss of all kinds.

- Physical loss, i.e. death of a loved one or destroyed property

- Environmental loss, i.e. moving, relocation, natural disasters that destroy the community

- Social loss, i.e. separation, divorce, intimate breakups, changing schools, being fired from employment

Grief has a physical impact on sleeping habits, appetite, concentration and physical illness. The release of stress hormones associated with grief can cause cardiac problems. Emotional reactions to grief are broad range — including anguish, sadness, anxiety, loneliness, and dejection. The experience of grief and loss causes a shift in overall ATTITUDE, OUTLOOK, AND PERSPECTIVE on life. In separation, divorce, and family transition some people consistently feel like something is missing in their life and they struggle to reestablish a comfortable identity and lifestyle in the face of the loss.

What are some things to be aware of when parenting a grieving child?

- Reluctance/Resistance to change
- Social anxiety, shyness
- Codependency/neediness
- Helplessness at times, perhaps gives up rather easily
- Pessimistic, easily disappointed, sadness
- Fear of disappointing others, anxiety
- Sensitive to rejection
- Lack of confidence, wavering esteem
- Prevalent ambivalence, falls into comfort zone and difficulty coming out of it
- Nonchalant, aloof, holding things in
- Somaticize, headaches, stomach aches
- Tendency to be misled, wants to believe people are good and honest or they may have a prevalent mistrust of others
- Adjusts best when situations are concrete and going as expected
- Responds well to consistent encouragement

Imani's comfort and understanding of a fatherly presence was beginning to take root as she was faced with the discomfort of separation anxieties and the experience of abandonment when the only father she knew moved away on her 11th birthday. I believe this, coupled with the prenatal experience of trauma and emotional anxiety experienced from my womb, contributed to many personal struggles through her adolescence.

I felt the constant need to reassure, motivate, encourage, and build her up — which was honestly quite exhausting. Sometimes I didn't feel like it. Sometimes I just wanted her insecurities to go away. Just when we got through one phase of apprehension or discomfort, something else crept in. Sports became a safe place for her. She found simple success through her athleticism in basketball and running track. We had an established family legacy of athleticism in our hometown, so it somewhat paved the way for her. I kept her involved in activities as much as possible, but I soon realized that I could not be her coach. Coaching and mommy-ing did not work for us.

Facebook Post: May 21, 2011

Ooo wee Father, please get her!! Did I really just tell my preteen that she "might be feeling a little b*tchy but I guarantee she can't match the HUGE b*tch I have inside of me?!?!" Hahahaha Lord scratch that...GET ME! LOL. But really kid...Don't get froggy!

*singin '*You Can't Win*' in my best MJ from The

As a former athlete with a profound tomboy-nature, I was a little too hardnosed for her fragile esteem. It was another area for us to bump heads and at that time in my life, I did not have a persistent capacity of patience. It takes a lot of patience and consistency to develop someone else's resiliency. I soon realized that she didn't need me to be her coach, she just needed me to be mommy. I thank God for the village of parents, friends, and loved ones who took the baton when I truly didn't have the energy or patience to do so. My brother, KJ, was great at picking her up for the weekend for some "uncle time." It gave us both a much-needed break from each other, to resume business as usual upon her return.

My youngest daughter, Erin, thrived in the presence of my father. Being that Janus and I were separated before her 2nd birthday, she was absent of any active memories of his presence. Her relationship with my father filled a void she likely didn't realize was there. They took walks together almost every day. Both girls grew up eating bowls of popcorn off his head while sitting on his shoulders watching cartoons. Night time rituals with Poppy were something they grew to love.

> ### Facebook Memory:
> ### January 11, 2011
>
> Sweetest thing ever…
> to see a little girl curl up in her grandfather's lap.
> *sigh*
> Thank God for my father.

I firmly believe that fostering stable family connections and replacement bonds are pivotal for a grieving child in the aftermath of separation and divorce. Moving in with my parents gave both girls a steady paternal figure to rely on and recreated the family feeling that dissolved with my divorce. I was really dedicated to making sure my children did not feel a lack of family togetherness.

Research and clinical experience has shown that one of the most crucial factors affecting children's responses to separation and divorce is neither the time spent with mom or dad, nor age, nor gender; but the quality of the relationship between the

> *In the case of an absent or estranged parent, fostering stable family connections and replacement bonds are pivotal for a grieving child in the aftermath of separation and divorce.*

parents during and after the separation period.[1] Children can be impacted by separation and divorce for several months to years thereafter, with the most traumatic and vicious divorces affecting children well into their adult lives. To minimize the negative effects of separation and divorce on children:

- **Practice open, honest communication about the changes they can expect, and the feelings involved.** Try to create as much continuity in their lives as possible.[1] In the case of transitioning between two

---

[1] Ofer Zur, "For The Sake of Our Children: Guidelines for Parents Undergoing Separation and Divorce," 2016. Retrieved March 1, 2018 from http://zurinstitute.com/sakeofourchildren.html

households, make the living spaces comfortable at both locations — with the input of the children where possible.

- **Protect the children from conflict.** That includes name calling, bad mouthing, intense arguing, and of course violence. Conversations that may incite conflict should happen outside of the children's reception. Do not use children as messengers, communicators, or spies because it creates an unnecessary burden on the children and may cause feelings of anxiety or guilt.[1]

- **Do not share the financial, custodial, or court battles with the children.** Young children should be assured the parents are working together for their best interest. Older children should have a sense their input is taken into account, but the final decision is in the hands of adults.[1]

- **Children respond to the adults around them.** If the parents can get on the same page, the children will respond accordingly. Parents must shift their communication style from marital-like to business-like, always considering the best interest of the children. Just because your ex was not a good spouse to you, it doesn't exclude them from being a good parent to your children. Differentiate those roles when making decisions. Consider counseling and/or mediation to address areas of disagreement — it may alleviate dispute in having a neutral party assist with decisions.

- **Close relationships are key**. Nearly all children feel as if they need to choose between their parents. It is best they have close relationships with both.[1] Parents should assure them that they can love both parents regardless of their primary residence. In the case of an absent or estranged parent, a replacement family figure is often helpful to fill the void — grandparent, aunt/uncle, etc. Be careful introducing a new significant other too prematurely.

- **Focus on the quality of time spent with the children, instead of the quantity of time, to alleviate the power struggle.** The separation-divorce process prompts intense conversations about custody and visitation in alternating days, weekends, weeks, holidays, etc. It may not be a 50-50 split; but every interaction had with the children through the separation/divorce process is an opportunity to ease the stress they may be experiencing. Make it count. Being consumed with the quantity of hours or days spent in comparison with the other parent may elicit frustration, resentment, and incite dispute, which your children will notice.

3

It's Complicated

Just as my life and thoughts were coming together, death struck once again—except now a lot closer to home. My uncle, married to one of my closest relatives, died of liver failure. Without knowing he was sick and living in a nursing home in New Jersey, I felt completely blindsided by the news. This left my closest aunt/grandmother-figure widowed after thirty-eight years of marriage, while managing health concerns of her own. She then relocated from their shared nursing facility to live with my parents, just around the corner from my house—the same two-bedroom condo that never sold years prior.

My aunt was twenty years older than my mother and father, and an elder maternal presence in the family. Her health deteriorated rather quickly in the last few

Dr. Melissa Tate-Scruse

months of her life, which resulted in a dedicated effort to care for her every need—bathing, feeding, grooming, etc. Not only did this add to the emotional toll of preparing for *seemingly* imminent death, it changed the dynamic of the relationships around her. At the age of eighty-one, in the aftermath of losing her husband, she had to depend on her loved ones, whom she ultimately considered her children, to address her every need. She was sick, tired, moody, irritable, withdrawn, and at times, downright mean. It was well outside of her typical silly, boisterous, independent, and proud personality, and therefore even more difficult to witness and experience. She was dying—emotionally and physically—anguished, confused, and struggling to allow us to care for her. The God-fearing spirit within her fueled the fight to the bitter end. Just days before her death, her refusal to take medication resulted in a Dixie cup mangled by her teeth marks. At nearly three o' clock in the morning, sleepless and weary from the last four weeks of caring for her every need, my mother and I were forced to hysterical laughter only to keep from crying. My aunt, more affectionately known as "Cat", had made herself very clear. She did not want that medicine.

I was still grieving from the previous December's suicide and the loss of my uncle when my aunt's journey on this earth ended almost two weeks shy of her birthday. She transitioned in peace, right there in my parents' home, lying in a hospital bed in my childhood bedroom. I was relieved to know her struggle was over, yet heartbroken and selfishly craving her presence. I stood at the podium in front of New Zion Baptist Church in Elizabeth, NJ with all my ambivalence, donning a royal blue suit jacket because she had recently told me I was" beautiful in that color". My heart was heavy, but my voice delivered her obituary just the same. Inside, I was angered by the loss within my family. I found myself haunted by memories of her deterioration, sleeping restlessly, tossing and turning to the sound of her yelling for us in the middle of the night. Even sadder was hearing her call her husband's name. As my "friend" and I were going through a breakup at the time, I couldn't help but wonder if I would have a lifelong love to cherish in that way. Grief compounded with grief. It was gut wrenching. I struggled to fully concentrate on daily happenings. I don't fully recall whether I was functioning as expected or not. It's kind of a haze to recall. I was anxious, and my spirit was in limbo. I found everyday laughter with my friends would give way to tears for no reason at all. I was raw with emotion, missing my "Kitty Cat".

This was all considered "normal" grief, but it felt complicated to me. I was struggling. My heart was so vulnerable and accessible. It hurt physically, emotionally, and spiritually. I had to fight the empty pain. I found solitude in a gospel music cd of hers — a collection of songs from Whitney Houston's Soundtrack of *The Preacher's Wife*, Marvin Sapp, and Kirk Franklin. The songs brought me to tears as much as it uplifted me. When my heart was heavy, I prayed to her directly, as one of my warring angels. My wrist is now tattooed with an homage of her initials above a haloed cat with angels' wings. She is always with me. I consciously decided to alter my thoughts from sadness and grief by re-familiarizing myself with pleasant memories of her—pictures, stories, thoughts, conversations, keepsakes, etc. I felt the need to disconnect the rapid deterioration of her final months from the lifetime of memories I had of her. I reminded myself of her smile, and her laughter, and her fun-loving spirit. I remembered playing *Sorry* and other games with her throughout my life. We spent countless holidays together and vacations in Las Vegas. I had thirty-four years of memoirs in my head and heart to recharge my spirit. And as the sadness lifted, I was lifted too. With each passing day, I resumed some degree of normalcy. But even now as I write, several years beyond her transition, my mixed emotions are still apparent. I feel blessed and grateful for her life, yet still bereaved.

As the turn of the New Year came and went, I stayed the course at the RTC, wondering if God just wanted me to sit still. My frenzied job search in the previous year did not yield any results and was derailed by the unanticipated responsibility of caring for my aunt. I resolved to my position there and was comforted by the familiar job setting and coworkers I considered family. We took care of each other through the crisis-oriented drama and suicide-related grief at the RTC, as well as through each other's seasons of personal milestones and missteps outside of the job—marriages, divorces, babies, miscarriages, health scares, triumphs/frustrations of parenting, relocations, resignations, sabbaticals, retirements, you name it. They were family.

I stopped job searching for a series of months, until my cell phone rang one evening in March. It was Dr. Allen, a psychiatrist I once worked with on the mobile crisis team in Baltimore City. We forged a friendship outside of work and kept up with each other from time to time, but I hadn't talked with her in years. The phone woke me up as I had drifted off to sleep watching television, but I was pleasantly surprised to hear from her. We took a moment to catch up, but ultimately, she called to offer me FREE use of her private office if I wanted to see some clients independently. *Self-employment?* Something leaped inside of me as I sat up in the bed. This had been encouraged of me several times in years prior by another colleague and school mate, but I often dismissed it because I was so accustomed to a steady paycheck and health benefits for my family. For whatever reason on this day, I was intrigued.

She said, "I'll give you about ninety days to pull it all together." I said, "Give me thirty!" As I hung up the phone, I called my school mate Kia, who had already been through this process. She guided me in a few steps, and by the end of the week I had developed a business profile, applied for a tax identification number, and secured professional liability insurance. A brief Google search led me to a long-awaited communication. After crafting a very professional "Hey, remember me?" email, I received a response the next day to schedule a thirty-minute phone interview, which brought my exit strategy from RTC to near-reality.

Email: Reconnecting 3/16/2011

Hello Dr. Harding;

You may or may not recall but we met under unfortunate circumstances over a year ago at [RTC]. As we discussed at that time, it seems we both walked away from our encounter feeling that it was not one of chance. You offered me an opportunity to fill a PT Clinical Supervisor vacancy at your agency, which I was evidently unable to take advantage of at the time. Most recently, I was able to visit your website and noticed a PT therapist position available. I am hopeful that you and I may be able to meet again with a different initiative in mind. With that said, I've attached my resume/CV for your review. Please feel free to contact me using the referenced information, as some information as changed since we last connected.

Thanks in advance for your time.

By the end of the month, I had begun seeing clients one evening a week at Harding Consulting, and slowly increased my caseload to include daytime hours, as I transitioned from full-time employment. I submitted sixty days' notice of resignation and began the administrative process to bill various insurance companies as the sole proprietor of my own private practice. By the close of the year, I had multiple streams of income as a contractual counselor and supervisor at Harding Consulting, while building my own practice out of offices in Laurel and Annapolis, Maryland. I was also an adjunct professor at my alma mater, Argosy University of Washington DC—teaching psychology classes to master's and doctorate students. My entire world shifted in the midst a stormy season of complicated grief, significant losses, and life adjustments. As various lives came to an actual death around me, I was working overtime to bring my life into balance after the "death" of a second marriage.

Relationship Status—*Complicated.*
Emotional Status—*Complicated.*
Mindset—*Hopeful.*

"If you're brave enough
to say goodbye,
life will reward you
with a new hello."

-Paul Coehlo-

4

Moving Beyond

Being the CEO, CFO, Director, Manager, and number one employee of my finances and fate, my motto was simple..." If I'm not working, we don't eat." Despite the near thirty-thousand dollar decrease in my income, I sincerely enjoyed my new mommy hustle from week to week—conducting outpatient therapy sessions, administrative billing of insurance companies, adjunct teaching on the evenings/weekends, and subcontract training and consultation. My work schedule was mine to design, therefore allowing more flexibility and freedom to balance out my life. It was quite a relief from the crisis-centered days at the RTC and I was steadily gaining a career presence in the DMV—the affectionately nicknamed DC, Maryland, Virginia area.

With yet another breakup under my belt, how does a single-divorced mother of two girls in her mid-thirties find a suitable counterpart? With no energy, time, or desire to frequent the latest hot spots, and the daily responsibilities of work and home in full-swing, the possibilities of finding a single, employed, good-looking, fun-loving, family oriented, responsible man felt slim to none. Through my dating woes, I often wound up settling.

✓ *Good-looking...check!* I'd be lying if I said this was not an important quality; although it has certainly gotten me into trouble. The handsome ones aren't always honorable, and cute isn't always committed. Sometimes, the best-looking ones are like kids in a candy store—wandering eyes, difficult to satisfy, with an insatiable appetite for sexy, and too cute for their own good—yes, even in their thirties. Being an athlete most of my life, I had a thing for athletic guys. Sports are a "limelight" activity in which ego, notoriety, and competition are all at the forefront. So, most of the guys I found attractive had ego issues and were accustomed to being the center of attention because of their athleticism. It made for some fidelity issues.

✓ *Employed...check!* Not too many grown men in their thirties are unemployed unless there's some extenuating circumstances. I was an equal opportunity dater—CEO's, school teachers, engineers, chefs, business men, professional athletes.

Some of them were flashy, *wine-and-dine* me types, but they were often particular in their ways, seemingly trying to keep up appearances. I found them extra-driven, borderline workaholics, which left little to no time for true commitment. Others were low-key, dinner and a movie types. This was a little closer to my laid back, down-to-earth personality, which brings me to my next point.

✓ *Family-oriented…sometimes!* I am SUPER family oriented. Most of my weekends consisted of family cookouts, card games, or attending Imani's seasonal sporting events (which could be an all-day affair). If your personality or desires couldn't merge into that dynamic, then our lifestyles were going to bump heads. My first marriage, heightened my understanding of men with their own family relationship issues. If he had relationship issues with his mother, father, children's mother, or his own children, it was bound to have an impact on our relationship in some way. It wasn't a deal breaker from the beginning, but it was a flag for concern. I once dated a man who had screaming, cursing disputes with his mother before extended periods of not speaking to each other. He blamed it all on her of course, and I gave him the benefit of the doubt until I saw otherwise. But I couldn't help but wonder how he was going to handle dispute and disagreement with me. It eventually came to pass. You guessed it—

yelling, cursing, blaming, silent treatment. It didn't last too long.

✓ *Single…sometimes*. You know the ones who want to keep the relationship discreet until "the right time." Or the ones who claim they have broken up with their ex, but they seem to disappear from texts or calls for hours or days at a time. Or the one who is open and honest about having a girlfriend/wife, but the relationship is on the verge of a perpetual breakup that hasn't quite happened. Yes, I admit it. I've settled for all these dudes.

At times, I was trying to turn a seemingly, well-packaged hoe into a husband. It doesn't matter how good of a woman you think you are, a male hoe has no intention of honoring you with complete commitment or fidelity, especially if you're giving up the cookies. I tried to convince myself that I was not looking for marriage, so just enjoy myself. But women are not built for casual sex. We are loving, emotionally driven beings with a built-in mothering instinct that gives us a central desire to love on others. I was hopelessly single and defeated in relationships, often compromising

> *It doesn't matter how good of a woman you think you are, a male hoe has no intention of honoring you with complete commitment or fidelity, especially if you're giving up the cookies.*
>
> -Dr. Melissa-

my time for company. My friends and family were getting married around me and I was genuinely happy for them. Despite my trials and tribulations with marriage and relationships, I was nobody's hater. I had a talk with God and figured… I guess it's time to get comfortable being single.

I was the eternal third or fifth wheel to my married friends and family. But I found contentment. I shed years of built up anger and resentment by merely focusing on myself and trying to be a better mom. My single mom goal was for "balance". I feared being an overworked therapist that spent too much time taking care of other people's children while neglecting her own. My prayer was for God to build me up so that when I met the man he had for me, I'd be prepared to love him. I had periods of abstinence through dating, which was a foreign concept in my circle. Even some of my friends asked, *"Girl you ain't giving up the cookies*??" One man who I refused for a sex specifically stated, "Selfishly, I wish you weren't so strong, but I get it." He and I both knew he was not able to give me the relationship I desired as he was going through relationship discontent of his own. There were other times that I gave up the cookies, my time, my energy, and my self-respect only to wind up with no true relationship to show for.

Having lackluster relationships was an area of shame and confusion I took on because I was raised under the auspices of a healthy, enduring marriage of middle school sweethearts. My parents' marriage was not perfect, and I'm sure there are gritty parts of their fifty-year love story I do not know; but I can say without question or hesitation that I was raised in a loving home with caring, supportive parents. Their relationship was one of comfort, laughter, and mutual affection. I never witnessed any dramatic arguments or emotional tirades between them. They showed us an endearing friendship and playfulness that makes me smile to this day. Truth be told, they made marriage look easy and seamless; so, I failed to understand why it was not as easy for me to find a life partner. At the end of the day, the blame game of pointing fingers at my dating choices and scrutinizing everyone else's problems was getting me no closer. Ultimately, I was led back to me. Without a better, improved, more insightful me; I wasn't going to have the relationship I desired.

Relationship status — Work in progress

Over the course of the next year, self-employment was flourishing, and the condo finally sold in a short sale. But an end-of-the-year review of my finances left me a little disenchanted. I felt content professionally, but there was no way I was going to thrive in Maryland's economy or housing market at that income. Despite the *doctor* title in front of my name, the Howard County area where I grew up was not built for a one-income/family of three household. It was a family-oriented suburb with great public schools, expensively located between Baltimore and Washington DC. It has been nationally recognized as one of the best places to live in the United States, but in that area, I would always be on the cusp of living with my parents. Although they were happy to have me, I distinctly recall the moment I realized I was too comfortable in their house. I began formulating ideas of knocking down a wall between my bedroom and the guest room to have my own living room/den suite. *That's absurd.* I did not want to live with my parents forever! I was in a financial quandary.

One January evening of 2012, I went to bed and woke up with a nagging idea, *"I think I'm moving to Charlotte"*. It was a strange thought, but somehow equally exciting. I had visited the North Carolina city on several occasions and fell in love with the University area at first. But after divorce, I had taken a few brief excursions there—hit Carowinds Amusement Park with the kids and hung out with my girlfriend Aretha and friends at the bowling alley. The cost of living was much more affordable than Maryland, yet it still reminded me of home. The fact that I had a love-interest in the Charlotte area made the thought that much more appealing. I began researching the public schools and job market, sending random emails to mental health agencies in the area, and seeking information about pursuing my professional license to practice mental health in the NC. Within 24 hours, I had my very first job lead! It wasn't long before I met with Dr. Rose LeDay to discuss joining her outpatient mental health practice, Transformative Life

Center (TLC). By the end of March, I completed a lot of research about housing, public schools, crime zones, etc. A 24-hour trip to Charlotte allowed me to meet with a realtor and look at five rental properties based on income projections and commute to work for TLC. Even though I visited all five properties, I was sold on the first one. It was a two-level, three-bedroom, three-bathroom townhome with a garage — located in a quiet subdivision with a pool in the sought after public school zone of Matthews-Mint Hill. I initially wanted something cheaper as not to stretch myself after the expense of relocation and starting a new job; but it immediately felt like a home for me and the girls. Still several hundred dollars cheaper than what I was used to in Maryland, I believed God wouldn't bring me all the way to Charlotte to have me falter. With no resistance or hurdles in sight, I signed the lease!

Despite my mother's tears of mixed joy and grief in anticipation of missing her only daughter and grandbabies, she said she was happy for me. My brother, father, cousins, and friends all expressed feelings of excitement for my decision and shared nothing but good energy leading up to my departure. This was especially important for the girls. Erin was only five years old and gearing up for kindergarten; but Imani was in full middle-school-swing, approaching eighth grade when we moved. She was reluctant to move away from the comfort zone of family and friends in Maryland, but I asked her to trust me because I believed more loved ones would join us in

Blessed Passenger

North Carolina over time. Something in my spirit told me this was the right move at the right time, and that it was just the beginning. As of June 2012, we were officially Charlotteans, merely six months after the initial decision.

We settled in to our new townhome rather simply. The condominium building back in Maryland became infested with bedbugs, so we had already gotten rid of all major furniture and personal belongings, down to the vacuum cleaner and television. The girls and I packed nothing but our clothes and our kitty cat, Onyx. I purchased a pub-style table/chair set, washer, and dryer from my landlord, which they left in place for us. The shiny dark hardwood floors and freshly painted walls were waiting for our personal touch. Groupon became my new best friend. I slowly but surely copped a bunch of deals on furniture, mattresses, and various décor items. Room by room the blank slates came to life.

We spent a lot of our first summer in Charlotte at the pool, playing video games on the Wii, and watching movies on Netflix. We took a few days to drive around the area, register for schools, and check out the local sites. During a day, it was easy to be invited to five different churches—which was a foreign concept to my kids. Now living in the "Bible Belt" of the southern US, Christianity and finding a "church home" seemed to be a common topic when people found out we were new to the area. Having been out of church fellowship for almost ten years, it was something I was willing to eventually consider, but my main goal was to get the girls

84 | *Blessed*

comfortable with their surroundings. It was a new and strange territory with strange, drawn out, southern accents. Their cousins and besties, CJ and Arionna, visited for a couple weeks. Aretha's daughter, Kaiya, hung out with the girls as well. The extra kiddies helped to keep them entertained.

My entertainment level was growing too! My bestie from the RTC, Sonja, called to catch up. I hadn't talked to her directly for some time since she had been living in North Dakota for her husband's last military assignment. He was now on the verge of retirement and they were considering Atlanta for a new home.

"What are you doing in Charlotte? My cousin has lived there for years. She loves it and keeps telling me to visit."

"And now I'm here, so you have to come!"
She and her hubby Steve came to visit for the July 4th holiday weekend. The girls and I met her at her cousin Kendra's house, whom I took a liking to right away. She lived near my new office in the Ballantyne area with her husband and two daughters. We laughed like school girls, played Rummi-Kub and Spades, and drank some cocktails. It was like old times — good family fun and good company. As the weekend ended, Sonja felt like she too could make a home in Charlotte — she joined us the following month.

Who would have guessed just a year prior we would be reunited in a brand-new city that neither of us ever considered living? I believe God makes things move that way. When you least expect it, something happens, and it seems it was supposed to be that way all along.

"True friendship
isn't about being inseparable,
it's being separated
and nothing changes."
-Anonymous-

Dr. Melissa Tate-Scruse

5

Order My Steps

"Hey Erin, what you been up to? What you been doin'?"

Saeed always called me by my middle name. Just the thought of him makes me smile. He is such a good dude. He always looked out for me in college—literally the overprotective college brother who showed up randomly to see if I went to class, to see who I was crushing on, or making sure I made it back to the dorm safely. We hadn't talked in years, but that didn't stop "big bro" from being all up in my face. He wanted the whole rundown.

"Erin, you're a doctor now? Wow! I'm so proud of you!" I continued to share that I recently recorded a television segment on a reality television show produced by We-TV. One of the show's producers randomly found me online and asked if I would be interested in performing a therapy session on camera. It was introduced to me as a Basketball Wives meets the black Kardashians type of show, in which one of the three sisters featured wanted to pursue counseling for some trust issues in her relationship. Rose gave me the green light to use the TLC office, and an all-day shoot went off without a hitch. Saeed gloated over me, but as always never ceased from challenging me. "Hey Erin, I was thinking...I saw this lady on Facebook who is kind of like a motivational speaker, talking about relationships and stuff. She posts these motivational videos and people follow her to hear what she has to say. You should do that. It would bring more notoriety and business into your office. Wifey has been writing blogs. Have you ever tried that? You could write about relationship stuff or different topics and post them through your social media for free advertising. Then you connect it back to your blog and website." I had already been in the process of building up my website — taking professional photos and getting it all fine-tuned. But I hadn't quite thought of writing a blog.

"What should I write about? Give me a topic."

"Ok, how about *'How Friendly is Too Friendly?'*"

"Ok, that's a good one. I'll come up with something and send it to you." About an hour later, after finishing up some clinical paperwork, I emailed him a draft. Apparently, I had a way with words because my phone rang five minutes later.

"YOOOO! You just wrote that off the dome?!" I literally LOL'ed. Saeed was so excited. "Yo, you're amazing! I can't believe you wrote it that fast. You need to be writing. I'm so proud of you!" I had long been admired for my writing skills. When writing poems, term papers, my dissertation, even clinical notes—my colleagues, professors, and supervisors were often drawn to my ability to articulate things and synthesize ideas or concepts. I did not realize it was such big a deal until I continued to progress professionally, and easily recognized writing was a struggle for others. Saeed was an intelligent guy—one of the smart ones. If he was impressed, it must've been worth the noise. I began writing a few blog articles, stocking them up for the big website launch. Once it was up and running, one of my first blog articles went viral!

May 2, 2014:
These Kids Are Getting on My Nerves!

Parenting is a catch-22. It's very cool to see a clone of your childhood-self take on the world. It allows you to reminisce about your childhood, compare their baby pictures to yours, and, regretfully, say all the things your parents used to say to you. I caught myself the other day saying, "If if's and buts were candy and nuts, it would be Christmas everyday" …UGH! That one is straight out of the mouth of Big Sam, my father, who is more affectionately known as "Poppy" to my children. What a sign of the times.

Kids have a lot of fun activities, like Little League sports, recitals, amusement parks, games and toys, etc. For years, my mother had a suntan from the wristband of her watch from summer after summer at my track meets. It wouldn't go away. These are the memories, rewards, benefits, and perks of the parenting program, but they come at a cost.

- Logistically, the hours and hours of practice to prepare for games and recitals is a part-time job, for which you pay to play. Some activities require travel (at your expense), which can occupy an entire evening and/or weekend. Vacations, ladies' night out, and date night with your boo are all put on the back burner during the season. It's often a daily commitment through the season, and it's exhaustive.
- Emotionally, the time and energy it takes to motivate your child when they are tired, burnt out, bored with the activity, or falling behind in their studies/chores is draining. It takes discipline, time

management, and dedication–from the child too. It's a teachable opportunity that a lot of child athletes, musicians, and dancers (eventually) appreciate and value in their adult years. But it's a long road to get there. It feels like work because it is.

- Financially, children are an open-ended mortgage with a variable pay scale. The demand is constantly changing, and it NEVER ends. It starts from the point of conception with medical bills and with each year, children have different financial needs. A huge economic milestone for a working parent is a child's transition to Kindergarten…that means no more day care bills. Therefore, I highly recommended living in a school district that you are happy with.

It's all in a day's work—there's literally twenty-four hours to get it all done. When the sun goes down and practice, school, and other activities are over, you still must feed, bathe, and clothe these little people! They want to watch TV, and they don't want to do the dishes, and they're afraid of the dark, and they don't want to go to school tomorrow, and they want the new fresh Jordan's, and their iPod is broken, and they want to have a sleepover with someone else's little person (whom you may or may not like) …and they want, and they want, and they want….

After the day is done, and I've managed all the dates, times, requests, and requirements, there's no way I'm wrong for wanting to shut my bedroom door and say, "THESE KIDS ARE GETTING ON MY NERVES! It's almost ten 'o'clock and Scandal is coming on! Just leave me alone!"

****

I love my children. Sometimes they make me belly laugh like Santa Clause on Christmas Eve. I am so proud to see my girls develop their own distinct personalities and conquer life's obstacles with each passing day. I am a mother, forever connected to my girls, biologically, emotionally, spiritually, and physically. They adore me! They want my love, hugs, kisses, attention, opinion, advice, laughter, sympathy, and sometimes pity. They want it from me because I am theirs and they are mine. It is a mutual attachment.

Now, brace yourself for the candor: Sometimes, I want them to go away. Not forever, but for a minute, or an hour, or a weekend, please! I want them to stop asking questions. I want them to take out the trash because it's full, not because I've asked. I want them to study hard and be their best on their own. Because sometimes I am not in the mood to give constant reminders and expectations to these kids. It gets on my nerves!

However, just as I have been candid, I must be equally as honest. I have no clue what I would be doing in my life without my children. A recent study suggests parents are happier than childless couples because there is greater meaning derived from life. In this respect, children add urgency and weight to personal life decisions that otherwise might be taken lightly. I have distinct, vivid recollections of conscious decisions I have made in my life because of my girls. Decisions in my relationships, in my housing, and in my career, have all been directly affected by my being a parent. So, despite the daily stressors of parenthood, the greater impact and obligation of someone being heavily attached and dependent on you is rewarding.

Closing thought: *They still get on my nerves*

I created and attached a PowToon's video to the article. Imagine three cute little screen beans of me and the girls on an average day. Much to my surprise, this blog article reached over 9,000 people in a week—shared, liked, and tweeted amongst hundreds and thousands. I was blown away. I had no idea that would happen. And to think it all started from a conversation with a long-lost friend who felt excited about my accomplishments and took the time to challenge me.

I continued to post a blog article every Friday from my website. Some of the articles were fun and friendly — others were more informative, or self-help driven. Either way, it seemed to fuel my creative juices, opening new avenues to express the thoughts and experiences that were on my mind. People seemed to respond to it positively. Little did I know it would pave the way for more opportunities.

****

"Hey Pal, it's your birthday! Let's go to dinner, my treat."

I had never in my grown years been referred to as "pal" until I met Tibby. She was one of the first friends I made upon moving to Charlotte two years prior. We met on the first day of school, bringing our daughters into Ms. Parrot's kindergarten classroom. It was a weird coincidence to find out she and her husband lived in my subdivision, just a few doors down the road from my townhome rental. Waiting for our girls to catch the school bus each morning, we laughed and giggled as if we were school girls — talking about our favorite TV shows, work, and family. Having her nearby was a nice reprieve from the hustle and bustle of managing work and parenting. The girls played for hours on a regular basis, which allowed us to chat the day away as well. She let me vent about the dilemmas of dating as a single mom, while she poured out her dilemmas of married life and a job she didn't like.

As we glanced through the menu at Azteca, surrounded by the sights and sounds of an authentic mariachi band, I could tell she was feeling some kind of way and really needed to talk. She was struggling in her marriage, feeling "stuck" and incomplete, tired of having the same conversations with her husband only to feel frustrated time and time again. It sounded all too familiar, "I get it. I've been there."

"What do you mean you've been there? You're so strong, handling your business. You have a career and you're taking care of the girls on your own. I'm not like you, Melissa"

"I guess I look strong now, but you don't know where I've been. I've had those dark, dead-end feelings too. I have a story to tell, I just haven't written it yet. You should come to this church with me in the morning." I had been going to Have Life Church for a few months. I was drawn to the "real talk" of the pastor. He preached in a way that people with real life struggles could relate. After being un-churched for about ten years, it was strange to find myself so eager to return week after week. "I really like it. It's an inviting church with a good word. It's not bougie. It's good for your spirit. Maybe it can help you sort out how you're feeling." We agreed on the details and I picked her up the following morning.

As we pulled up in the parking lot, we were greeted by various people. Nearly every ten feet, someone was waving and welcoming us with a warm hug and smile. Tibby's introverted tendencies were kicking in as we approached the sanctuary, "Good Lord all these hugs! I ain't used to all this." I tried to prepare her for that, but you don't fully understand it until you're there. We chuckled as we were ushered to our seats during praise and worship time. We sat a few rows back, centered in front of the pulpit, as Pastor Shomari White was a midst a series titled "Where's Your Faith?"

When he took his position on the altar to begin the word, he proceeded to speak over the congregation about how fears are educated into us, and that we should never be afraid to try something new because *"beginners built the [Noah's] ark and experts built the Titanic."* He preached from 2 Kings, Chapter 4 about the poor widow who owed taxes in the aftermath of her husband's death. He was one of the sons of the prophets, well known to the king and he had the reputation of a God-fearing man worthy of honor. But he died poor and in debt more than he was worth; and the widow feared her sons would be taken into slavery as debtors. She complained that she had nothing in her home to give and had overlooked a small jar of olive oil. King Elisha prophesied she borrow an abundance of empty vessels from her neighbors and pour the overlooked blessing of oil into them. The small jar flowed miraculously and endlessly as long as she had an empty vessel to receive it. When the vessels were full, it ceased.

She was then able to sell the oil for money, relieve the debt, and live (both she and her sons) off what was left.

As the sermon continued to unfold, Pastor Sho asked us all, "*How much do you think God can do? Have you overlooked the blessings of the Lord? Are you tapping into what God has already given you? Perhaps you've been asking God to bless your finances or your career, but you've overlooked what He has already given you.*" The energy in the room was steady climbing, as heads were nodding in agreement and people began to shout back. He went on to discuss the "Kairos Collision," the moment where God moves, encouraging us to tap into the gifts God has given us, so the blessings of the Lord can flow miraculously and endlessly in our lives. Then he said, "*I don't know who this word is for, but somebody in here has a book to write.*" I instantly felt a Kairos Collision in my gut. I was in awe, recalling the words that slipped off my tongue less than 24 hours before in that Mexican restaurant. Tibby turned her head and bright eyes in my direction, and we stared at each other in amazement. "*Ok God, I hear you.*"

We both left church that September morning, filled with joy and excitement. That afternoon, I began outlining my personal story of toxic relationships—a story that eventually developed into my book writing debut, *Blind Passenger*. I had always been well received as a writer, from high school through college. I previously tossed around the idea of writing a story about my first marriage and divorce; but after writing a few pages, it sat dormant on my computer for years. On the heels of one of my first blogposts going social media viral, reaching thousands across the country, I was asking God to bless my finances, family, relationships, etc. I was guilty of overlooking the writing gift and the story he was walking me through. "Where is your faith," he asked. "Steady climbing," I thought to myself.

Writing *Blind Passenger* was an amazing process. Firming my walk with God and attending Have Life Church on a regular basis opened my spirit to revealing all the gritty details involved in my two failed marriages. It also enlightened me to the connection between my childhood sibling issues and unresolved anger and forgiveness that was lingering in my heart. Writing the book became a liberating process as I was forced to re-read old journals, emails, and letters to revisit my state of mind through some of the darker days of my life. There were only a couple of close friends and family members that knew some of the events of my past, but there was not one person who could claim to know all the details. I initially began writing the book in secret. It wasn't until I was nearly completed that I shared the news with a couple of friends (Sonja and Tibby included), and eventually family. I realized that in writing my story, I was also sharing parts of their story; so, I gave them the appropriate courtesy. They were receptive and supportive throughout—especially my mother. She certainly had her difficulties over the years with bearing the cross of a drug-addicted son, but she never hesitated for a moment to support my truth.

Blessed Passenger

Although I appeared to have it all together on the outside, I continued to crave a viable romantic relationship. My dating dilemmas hit a brick wall when a series of hopeful prospects seemed to fizzle out for several reasons. All in all, I found myself confronted with the same issues—dating non-committal playboy types who like their cake and eat it too, or narcissistic-jealous types that want everything their way, or perhaps they were good, dudes-but they just weren't for me. I had not been having casual sex with anyone, but after reconnecting with a hometown friend on Facebook who said all the right things of marriage and commitment and relocating to NC, I put the cart before the horse. His jealous insecurities and mood swings eventually rose to the surface as some of my professional endeavors began to take off. I might as well have reunited with my first ex-husband. After four months of long-distance phone calls, Skype sessions, and visits, the relationship came to a screeching halt when he accused me of having affairs with my television producer, my pastor, my nephew, and with his cousin (whom I've never met). Insult to injury: In my annual physical exam, I tested positive for the Human Papilloma Virus, a sexually-transmitted infection associated with causing cervical cancers. I thought to myself, "*I am too old for this crap.*" I made a promise to God that the next man I had sex with would be my husband. I didn't care if it took me five, ten, or twenty years. I wanted God's best for me in every area of my life. I was fully resolved to a life of celibacy — not halfway resolved or somewhat considering or only celibate while single — but fully resolved to remain single and celibate until marriage.

> ### 1 Corinthians 6: 18b-19
> "For sexual immorality is a sin against your own body. Don't you realize that your body is the temple of the Holy Spirit, who lives in you and was given to you by God? You do not belong to yourself..."

If marriage was in God's cards for me, then I had to honor myself, my body, and my mind. And ultimately, I had to honor God by showing high regard for the body, the temple, he gifted me. Pastor Sho preached fervently on healthy relationships and healthy dating; which served as a kind of accountability.

For the first time in my life, I was firmly committed to a church body — praising, worshipping, tithing, and thirsting for a relationship with God. After less than a year at the church, I began serving with the Ushers/Greeters Ministry. I adapted to it like a fish does to water. I fell in love with my church and my pastors; and I was proud to be raising my children in the church. It fortified the foundation of our family. Turning into an avid church-goer like never before, Sonja began to inquire what I liked about the church, *"Are there any cuties in there?"* To which I firmly declined, *"Girl, boo! Most of the men at church are either married or seem a little gay!"* We hollered laughing together. *"I just love the church. It's a good word."*

It wasn't long before those words came back to bite me in the butt. I consistently noticed a handsome gentleman praying for people at the altar. I didn't know his marital status, but I didn't see a wedding ring on his finger. As church released each Sunday and Wednesday, he was often conversing with lots of people, seemingly popular in the church. I never saw him romantically connected or engaged with any women. From what I could tell, he was a single dad with three young daughters. Week after week for several months, I noticed him, noticing me, noticing each other—smiling, waving, checking me out.

One Sunday in July 2015, he approached me with a tray of cupcakes and a business card. Apparently, his name was Anthony and he was preparing for the grand opening of his custom cake design business. I was immediately impressed with his cake artistry—cakes that look like Jordan's and purses and other mega-cakes you see on Food Network. It was nice to finally put a name with the handsome face I had been seeing for several weeks. After a few Facebook "likes" and continued glances in each other's direction, we began talking on the phone. I told him I may need a cake for a book signing event (this was before *Blind Passenger* was published). We talked about church, family, sports, business, you name it. Once we started talking, we never stopped. This dating experience was like no other I had before. He was super funny, open, honest, and firmly committed in the church. He was a single father with three daughters, separated from his wife, approaching divorce; yet he still felt called to marriage. He too, was living a single, celibate lifestyle after a separation, divorce, and failed engagement.

Pastor Sho preaches about relationships every August, so the timing of introducing ourselves and getting to know each other couldn't have been more perfect. It was like an accelerated speed dating course. Every week, we had new relationship discussions to explore and dive into. The sermons were so rich in a mixture of "real talk" backed up with scripture. Together, we reviewed recommended reading of Dr. R.A. Vernon's *Ten Rules of Dating* and Gary Chapman's *The 5 Love Languages*. It seemed like God ordered my steps to Have Life Church in such an intentional way. It was as if he was giving me a playbook as an answer to my love life prayers. It was unbelievable how perfectly matched we were for each other. So perfect that it felt too good to be true. On one hand I was super excited, head over heels for Anthony. On the other hand, was this nagging voice in the back of my mind that it wouldn't work out, yet again. Not because of anything he was demonstrating, but because my history of failed relationships was evidence that it could happen again. I also had a strange, but comforting, feeling the Have Life Church family was as protective and worried about his heart and his children, as my family and friends were worried about my heart and my children.

The Lord began to deal with me, confronting me in my dreams, about issues with trust. Although I thought *Blind Passenger* was a completed work ready for editing, I was awakened from my sleep at approximately 3 o'clock in the morning with *Proverbs 3:5-6* bouncing around my mind. Although I had been attending church regularly, I was not at the point of spouting out Bible verses. I didn't know what the verse was, but I had a nagging feeling it was about trust. I reached for my bible to look it up. It read: *"Trust in the Lord with all your heart, do not rely on your own understanding. Acknowledge him in all that you do, and he will direct your path."* My heart leaped inside. I had not had a spiritual experience like that before — awakened from my sleep with such a profound message as I was beginning to worry about this new relationship that felt too good to be true! Even further, I was feeling inclined to incorporate the scripture into my book writing somehow. It actually became a catalyst for continued editing and chapter growth that I now look back upon as necessary additions for developing the overall message of *Blind Passenger*. After writing for several hours and falling back to sleep with a new sense of spiritual confidence and accomplishment for the book, I woke up around 9ish to find *Proverbs 3:5-6* as the daily reading in my Bible app. Eerie, weird, crazy, right?? — perhaps not for one who has been walking in Christ all their life. But for someone like me, who was fairly new, yet firmly decided about a new life direction, I was in awe! From that point on, it seemed this scripture would show up in the most unexpected places as if God himself was trying to tell me, *"Yes it happened. Yes, it's real. Yes, I'm talking to you."* This type of "coincidence" heightened my spiritual awareness and I continued to experience dreams and coincidental messaging that drew me closer in relationship with God. In the following weeks of courtship with Anthony, I had another dream that resembled a hazing crucifixion ritual. I was in a dark dungeon-like area, chained and bound, surrounded by cloaked figures with no faces. I was sobbing uncontrollably, faced with fear of what seemed like my approaching death. With a crown of thorns on my head, I was being led to the cross. Despite my fear, sadness, and anxiety of what was to occur, I cried out, "I trust you completely Lord! I surrender to you!" And I immediately woke up. I am by no means a dream interpretation specialist, but it rings pretty clear to me that the Lord was looking for me to stop worrying and surrender to his will. Surrender can be scary. It requires so much vulnerability and a willingness to just allow life to unfold knowing that God will not let you falter beyond his repair.

So, I continued in the journey to trust God, trying to give in to my reluctance and fears, and he continued to show up. One August/September night, while I was hanging out in the bakery with Anthony, hours of laughter and conversation shifted to my being plagued with worry that our relationship would not always be this way. It wouldn't always be joy and happiness — *remember Melissa, you've had this before and it failed*. I completely withdrew into my head and stood there in silence. He was initially distracted with decorating a cake, but soon noticed that I was super quiet and had disengaged from conversation. He came to me, asking me repeatedly what the matter was. I didn't have the words. I just lowered my head and stood there as my eyes welled up with tears. Anthony wrapped his arms around me and rubbed my back, whispering in my ear, *"Whatever is bothering you is not your thoughts. I don't know what's wrong but I'm going to hold you until you're ready to talk."* As I began to boo-hoo cry like a baby, I was given a vision of the two of us standing in our church lobby. He was standing at the bookstore window with his back to me several yards away, as a light shone down on me from above and lit a pathway toward him. I was blown away! These are all completely new experiences to me. After I collected myself from tears, I told him about the vision. He was just as stunned as me. In all my years, at that time approaching thirty-nine years old, I had never received such pivotal messaging from God. It affirmed my commitment to Him, shed the anxieties I had about my relationship with Anthony, and continued to heighten my spiritual awareness.

"Never be afraid to trust an unknown future to a known God."
- Corrie Ten Boom -

6

Kingdom Dating

Despite the strong spiritual connection between Anthony and me, life was still in full swing around us. He was a busy entrepreneur, single-dad of three girls, trying to jumpstart his own store front bakery; while I was raising my two girls trying to build a private practice and had recently ventured into radio and television recording. Despite it all, we were like two high school kids getting to know each other, laughing and talking to the wee hours of the morning. We were both very candid about our past relationship woes. There was no stone left unturned—

emotional abuse, physical abuse, infidelities, sexually transmitted diseases, legal issues, financial struggles, spiritual discussions, alcohol/drug use, pornography, masturbation, and sexuality issues. Everything was revealed.

We established a solid commitment from the beginning that honest and open communication was going to be at the foundation of our relationship. After having been through so much as individuals, we were each so willing to be one-hundred percent transparent about who we have been, how we came to be, and where we were trying to grow. One thing that really drew me in was his willingness to accept accountability for some of the difficulties and misunderstandings that occurred in his previous marriage. He divorced and married his ex-wife twice, wanting to keep their family together; but ultimately the damage of poor communication, emotional infidelity, and mistrust was done. Through the process, they found themselves maturing in different directions.

Anthony was firmly rooted in church and fully invested in growing his business; and therefore, focused the bulk of his energy in those endeavors. I admired his impeccable talent for cake design and was even more touched by the obvious bond he had with his girls. It was common to see them clung to his side in the church lobby or chasing him around trying to hug on him. Daddy's girls without question. It is quite special to see little girls love and enjoy spending time with their dad. I had the same type of relationship with my father. My dad was a

Blessed Passenger

rough-n-tumble, playful type of dad. He coached me in nearly every sport I played, taught me how to fish and ride a bike and how to take care of my car. Even as adults, we sit back and discuss sports, our years of coaching track together, and old hometown friends—so, I can relate to being a daddy's girl. Unfortunately, I had not afforded either of my daughters the same experience with their biological dads in the aftermath of divorce. Their dads were estranged and chose not to make themselves available for reasonable visitation. In that respect, my father was the most consistent fatherly presence they knew, in absence of their own dads. He was there for track meets, dance recitals, basketball practices, Donuts for Dads, field trips, birthday parties, bedtime stories, breakfast rituals with "Poppy", and so much more. My dad was the closest thing to a "daddy" they knew. So, Anthony's positive interactions with his girls was pivotal, and likely indicative of how he would interact with my girls.

Pastor Sho always says, "examine the fruit," meaning the evidence of someone's demeanor and being is often right before your eyes. If a tree was bearing rotten fruit, you would not eat it. At this point, Anthony was not demonstrating any major vices or "rotten fruit" to bring concern. I felt like I was dating a male version of myself— funny, athletic, grounded, driven, easy to talk to, loving, honest, celibate, and maturing on purpose. There was no confusion about the intentions of our dating. We had discussions of marriage very early—which was scary, but seemingly appropriate at the same time. A blended family in this capacity is not what I imagined in my wildest dreams, yet I was faced with the potential reality of being the mother of five girls. I'm sure God was laughing enthusiastically at me—the tomboyish, daddy's girl who liked to run, jump, and ball—not a son in sight. I was laughing at myself.

The blending of personalities and interactions between the seven of us went eerily well. There was obviously some initial hesitation and uncertainty about what to expect, but for the most part we bonded in our playfulness—having family game nights, dancing on the Wii, playing board games, watching movies together, playing tag/football/basketball in the park, going hiking, and just getting to know each other. During one of my favorite bonding moments, we sat around a bonfire on the back porch, making s'mores, asking and answering thought provoking questions of each other. It was great, purposeful conversation—an activity we still enjoy from time to time. We kept our relationship on the low for the first month or so, until we were certain where things were headed. Before long, it was fully public to our church friends and family. People marveled at our connection and how the girls seemed to get along. One uncanny circumstance is how my youngest, Erin, was often confused with his youngest daughter. Approximately eleven months apart in age, similar height, same naturally curly twists, and little brown faces—we started calling them "the twins." It turns out they were already friends in children's church before Anthony and I started dating. God is funny in that way.

By late-September, our relationship was going strong, but Anthony was amidst some financial struggles. In his transition from running a bakery business out of the house with some side-contract work in construction and home improvement, to opening the storefront, his money was tight. The downshift from a two-income household to a single income is not for the faint of heart. He was now going through the stages of divorce-related grief and life-altering changes in personal identity that I experienced several years prior. I could obviously identify with this season of uncertainty and stress. All the signs were pointing to a need for him to let go of the house he was living in because he was behind on the rent and barely making ends meet. Thank God for the mercy of a landlord that appreciated him as a man and a generally responsible tenant, because he was pretty much near-homelessness. He did not have the family support in NC as a fall back plan like I had when I lived in MD. Furthermore, letting go of the house meant letting go of his girls' primary residence for schooling jurisdiction. Luckily, their mother had recently moved into the same district—Ann is the only child that would be assigned to a new school with the change of residence to her mother's address. But emotionally, having been a stay at home dad, home school teacher, and primary caregiver for his girls—he was heartbroken to consider moving in this direction.

Over the course of several weeks, I helped Anthony with purging and packing up the house. The Stephenson's, our friends from church, were happy to offer him a rest haven through the transition. His belongings were stored between their garage and mine, while the girls took primary residence with their mother. All the while, conversations of marriage became more realistic and the option to move in with me was explored. I offered my home to him and the girls, making whatever adjustments were required. Reorganizing bedrooms for additional sleepers was in full effect during custodial weekend visits.

Things happened so quickly that I didn't take the time to explain it all to my family, who was scheduled to visit in the coming weeks. They knew about Anthony and my new dating relationship, but I did not explain the depth of it all—nor the fact that he had *kinda, sorta* moved in. That all came to a head one afternoon as my parents and I were sitting on the couch. They looked at each other and me in surprise as Anthony came in the front door using his own key…*Awkward*. My mother coyly asked, *"So what exactly is going on here?"* I just smiled with shy excitement, *"Uhhhhh, I'm keeping him."* I admit it wasn't the best introduction, but this connection was difficult to explain unless you saw it with your own eyes. I was reluctant to share how convinced I was about this relationship because of my history of moving too fast in my previous relationships. I just wanted my parents to see for themselves what I was experiencing. By the end of their visit, they recognized him with honorable intentions. They liked him immediately. They found him respectful, and of course super silly. They could see our love and laughter on the surface, and ultimately how well he interacted with all the girls; hence, stamp of approval.

After a few weeks of cohabitation, our initial vow of celibacy until marriage fell by the wayside. In this day and age, premarital sex is quite the norm and something both of us were accustomed to in previous relationships. We rested on the idea that we were *committed to be married anyway* as we waited for his divorce to be final; but somehow something about it didn't feel quite right. Following the Thanksgiving Holiday, we scheduled an appointment with Pastor Sho. He had been watching us over the past couple months—particularly the interactions between the girls. He too was surprised to see the blending of personalities and positive interactions between the five of them. He asked a lot of questions to understand us individually, and as a couple. By the end of the hour, he gave our relationship his blessing with one exception—he discouraged us from continued cohabitation and premarital sex until we were married. We all prayed together, and the session concluded.

As Anthony and I returned to the house, we processed the course of our meeting with Pastor, and completely understood where he was coming from. We pretty much violated our commitment to celibacy, yet asked the man of God to bless us anyway. That's out of order. We were now faced with developing a new plan for Anthony to move out of the house. This left us both feeling uneasy, as my girls, Imani and Erin, had grown accustomed to his presence in the house over the past month or so. We were also in the routine of co-parenting and weekly visitation for his three girls—Gizelle, Janese, and Ann. Although it was going well in most respects, there had been so much adjustment and transition going on—it was heart wrenching to think about downshifting the family progress we made thus far. This was a tough pill to swallow. Anthony and I each went into heavy prayer about it.

On top of my worries about the family transition, I was still wrestling with my own sexuality. There was admittedly a part of me that was bothered by the thought of not being able to have sex with my future husband. Even though I understood the concept, there was a selfish part of me that felt like—*I've been waiting for this type of love my whole life and now that it's here, I have to wait??* I was aggravated. I literally got on my knees in prayer asking God, *"What is this aggravation? Why do I feel so annoyed when I know I'm wrong?"* I stayed in this prayer posture until I heard from God. I wept with gratitude for what he gave me. I felt a sense of enlightenment over me and I immediately went into journaling.

Journal Entry:
Sexual Revelation (12/08/2015)

Today I experienced a sexual revelation. As God has gifted me with the most genuine and sincere experience of love that anyone could ever ask for, I have allowed my HUMAN SENSE OF ENTITLEMENT to taint what God has intended for me. For so long, I've been programmed, groomed, and guided to allow for sexuality in my relationships as a demonstration of love and as a tool to receive intimacy. And although this may be true in marriage, it has been taxed in the human worldly mind. Sex has been used prematurely as a false sense of belonging in a relationship that lacks true and intended Godly love. Lustful urges have become common place, acceptable, and a commended form of communication in relationships that are ultimately lacking true love and intimacy...and ultimately lacking God. In seeking wise spiritual counsel for the direction of our relationship, I was redirected from engaging in premature sex with Anthony before we were married. We were encouraged to refrain from living together to minimize the temptation and natural tendency to act upon our sexual energy for each other. It didn't sit right with me. I was plagued with uneasiness at the thought of stepping back from what God has shown me is for me. Although I recognize my iniquity for premature sex, my spirit was unwilling to refrain from cohabitation. I felt like my connection with Anthony was misunderstood and minimized. I collapsed in prayer...

THEN GOD... in prayer, I confronted my transgressions and sense of uneasiness. I asked for forgiveness, clarity in my thoughts, and order to my steps. "I TRUST YOU GOD, I TRUST YOU GOD, I TRUST YOU GOD. I SUBMIT TO YOU. WHAT IS THIS UNEASINESS? WHAT IS THIS CONFLICT IN MY MIND? WHAT IS THIS I FEEL?" I was gifted with clarity and revelation...I've been plagued with a human sense of entitlement for sexuality in a loving relationship, a relationship that is not sealed in marriage. With this revelation I was able to ask God to restore the dark places of sexuality inside of me...the areas of me that naturally allowed my sexuality to open up in an attempt to give/receive love and intimacy. I asked God to restore the sense of entitlement I have in my mind that says *I can have sex because I am in love*. Those are thoughts of human nature....

BUT GOD expects you to rise above to reap the harvest of kingdom love he has for you. God has the power to put his Super on your natural and transcend the human sense of entitlement to sex in relationships. "I call on you God to enter those dark, distorted, broken parts of my human sexuality so that I may receive the kingdom relationship you have for me. I ask for your Super to transcend my natural human thoughts of sexuality, in order to bring the blessings to pass.

As you have gifted me a true, sincere, genuine, Godly love and affection, I no longer need to hold onto the human sense of entitlement for premature sex and intimacy. I can give it to you, exchange my human yoke for your Superhuman yoke, and rise above the seemingly impossible [cohabitation without sex] until this union is truly blessed and legally recognized in Holy Trinity. Yessss God! Thank you, God!

And that was that. Anthony and I met with Pastor in the following days. We shared our concerns about opening wounds of abandonment and uneasiness if we forced the family system to adjust to another housing change — to which he concurred, but again asked us to honor the vow of celibacy. The three of us stood in prayer and agreement to fortify the bonds of our blending family and to refrain from premature sexuality until we were married. With nothing but profound obedience and honor, we kept our covenant with God and Pastor Sho.

Anthony and I continued to keep prayer in the forefront of our relationship. During an afternoon of personal Bible study diving into the relationship of Adam and Eve, I began to read heavily into the definition of a "help meet". The Bible says, "it is not good for the man to be alone; I will make him a help meet for him." I stayed in prayer — *Lord let me never forget that I am here to help him. Strengthen me, shape me, mature me to be the helper you need* me to be for him. I will honor this relationship for the rest of my days knowing that it has come from you. I will not marry again. Without pause, the Lord interjected—*You will never divorce again.* Good Lord! I cannot impress enough how important prayer and conversation with God has become in my life. The revelation and wisdom that is given to me in those moments is amazing!

There was no doubt in my mind that God had truly been working on me. The natural ideas and ways of life I was accustomed to were becoming useless to me as I began to accept more Godly, spiritual beliefs and customs. Your beliefs are a reflection of your mindset—which then paves the way for your actions and demeanor. In developing a stronger belief system and understanding for Christ, my mindset was steadily maturing to embrace a healthier, more spiritual lifestyle. Through much fasting and prayer, I shed my cravings for wine and continued to work on that unbridled foul mouth of mine. As the following spring approached, it was a no-brainer to sign up for water baptism and the required baptism classes.

Baptism is an outward demonstration of an inward transformation, and I was surely being transformed—past hurts, indiscretions, poor choices, and various temptations. I was ready to wash it all away. On Easter Sunday 2016, despite the spring showers and chill in the air, I stood in the baptismal pool with Pastor Sho, my spiritual father, and Deacon Anthony Scruse, my future husband. As Co-Pastor Jacque finished reading the baptismal declaration over the microphone, they dunked me backwards into the water and released me forward to the cheers of my children, my true-blue sister friend Sonja, and my entire Have Life Church family. *Second Corinthians 5:17 NLT This means that anyone who belongs to Christ has become a new person. The old life is gone; a new life has begun!*

In the following month, Anthony and I were engaged and officially married. It was a small ceremony of less than fifty—mostly composed of our church family and friends. Sonja, Tibby, and my parents were ever-faithful cheerleaders, as expected. Despite our relocation to Charlotte several years before, the presence and support of my parents was unfailing. For track meets, dance recitals, field trips, birthday celebrations, holidays, and now a wedding—my mom and dad have been such a remarkable presence in everything we have done. Sitting on the

> **Facebook Memory:**
> **April 30, 2016**
>
> Today I married the most amazing companion, friend, and partner for life. He is a Godly man who makes me laugh and smile bright enough for the heavens to see. He loves on me and my babies, and pours life into us, individually and collectively, LIKE NO OTHER.
> I choose him. I adore him, and I will honor him until death do us part.
> Thank you, God!

front row just before the altar of Have Life Church, Dad pronounced his "giving away" and Pastor Sho officiated the marital blending the Tate-Scruse family.

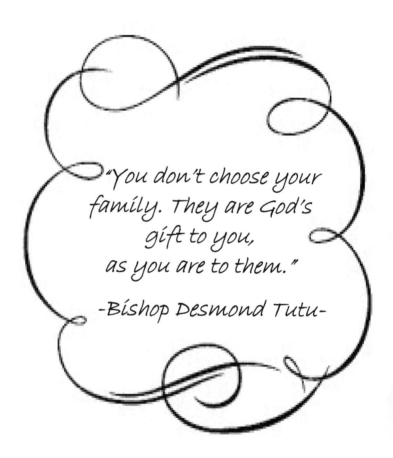

"You don't choose your family. They are God's gift to you, as you are to them."

-Bishop Desmond Tutu-

7

#DaddysGirl

As we are faced with the death of a loved one, our turmoil becomes a billboard for the world to see. Hearing the news of death has a way of punching you directly in the gut—physically, emotionally, and spiritually—and we are immediately thrust into a broken image of our "normal" self. It is as if time stands still for an absolute second as you process what you've been told. Then, everything that lost loved one was or is to you is ripped from your being, and you crumble. Some people fall out, they literally lose strength, control, and stability of their legs—falling into the arms of others or falling to the ground in anguish. It's the body language of instant grief that has our shoulders slouched, head hung low, and our arms and hands folded in, as tearfulness, sobbing, and sometimes screams come pouring out of us. There are moments of disbelief, numbness, and shock as you try to wrap your mind around the loss. Your thoughts are racing with memories of that person, or of recent events or conversations with that person, or perhaps the details that led up to their death, as you try to understand why and how this happened.

This was me. On August 31, 2017, I awoke around six o'clock in the morning to a text message from my sister-in-law Ericka, which she had sent just before midnight: "Hi sis. Mom just called an ambulance for your dad. He is having chest pains, shortness of breath." My dad had been diagnosed with Type 1 Insulin-Dependent Diabetes for over thirty-five years—now sixty-eight—it had certainly taken a toll on him over time. In 2006, kidney failure led to dialysis and organ transplant at the donation of my brother, KJ. It was a blessing to see two men I honor and hold so dear, support each other through the recovery process. My father did not fully rebound to his prior muscle-bound, spry physical energy, but his zest for life and love for his family never failed. He spent his retirement years alongside my mother, his companion of fifty-five years, leisurely visiting casinos and spending time with his grandchildren, both in Virginia and North Carolina. Perpetually known as Poppy, he was an ever-present playmate and jokester with the kids. He also continued to work with the State of Maryland's Athletic Association of high school athletics, managing and officiating track meets. He was highly regarded in the track and field industry, having coached and mentored hundreds of athletes to state championships, national recognition, and collegiate success. Despite the looming responsibility of managing his eating habits, blood sugar, and cholesterol from day to day, his dedication and ability to inspire others did not falter. His doctors had recently been considering a surgical implant for insulin regulation. But on this morning, the dilemma was chest pain and shortness of breath. I was confused. After a few phone calls to family with no response, I rolled from my bedroom pillow to my knees at bedside. Amidst my prayers, Ericka returned my call to give me the details, of which there was no immediate alarm. After finishing my prayers, I went to the treadmill for my morning workout. I posted a group message on Facebook to my *Staying Power* accountability group as a means to inspire.

> So.... I'm a daddy's girl. Always have been, always will be. I woke up this morning with a text from my sis that dad was rushed to the hospital for chest pain and shortness of breath. After calling everyone and getting no response, I took a moment to pray. By the time, I finished praying my sis called to say he's stable, coherent, never lost consciousness, but was admitted to the hospital for testing. So...I pray some more...for healing angels, restoration, recovery, and thank God for his protection. Next stop: treadmill.... halfway through my walk/jog intervals my mom calls. I slowed the treadmill to 3 mph and got the update from her. Things are well but still running tests to make sure there's no blood clots or anything. After the call, I ramped up to 6.5 mph and ran ½ mile. So altogether 20 min workout for 1.5 miles, still praying, in spite of it all. #Daddysgirl

I could have easily let my worries or concerns about my father derail my motivation to work out, but I pressed on without excuses. There was an eerie peace over me.

By the end of the hour as I was getting out of the shower, I heard my phone ringing. It was KJ with the dreaded news — the phone call I will never forget. The pain, tears, and anguish in his voice as he could barely breath, let alone form the words to say *"Missy, Dad's gone."* I have replayed this moment in my mind a thousand times because it felt so unreal. It felt like something I had seen in a movie before, but it was me. I fell to the floor with my towel barely wrapped around me, screaming, *"What? No, No, No!"* over and over again. As a whirlwind of thoughts, memories, and emotions were taking over me, I kept shaking my head in disbelief. As much as I wanted to believe this was a terrible dream or a misunderstanding, the reality of my father's death was heavy and haunting. Its reported that his blood pressure bottomed out and his heart arrested. They were unable to resuscitate him after nearly an hour. Despite his normal joking and lighthearted demeanor just a few hours before, he passed away.

I called my husband frantically, just needing someone to be with me. He was already at work, as I sat there on my bedroom floor alone, sobbing, shaking my head, trying to figure out what to do next. I cried like a baby, like a daddy's girl, in disbelief. My last moments and conversations with him began to flash before my eyes. We had just spent four days together at Erin's National Dance Championships. Me, my parents, and the girls walked around downtown Charleston, went to the beach, and enjoyed the local food. He was winded from all the walking, sometimes quiet. His pressure bottomed out and we had to call an ambulance from the beach. He was released within a few hours, but wait---*should I have known this was going to happen?* Oh God, no. I wasn't ready for this. I was troubled with grief and already mourning his absence.

My mind was racing with a thousand thoughts. And my heart grew increasingly heavy with sorrow as I thought about my mother (his life partner of over fifty years), my oldest brother Pure (who was at the moment incarcerated), and Imani (who had just gone away for her freshman year of college). She and Erin were losing the most consistent fatherly presence they had known in absence of their biological fathers. I worried how Pure would receive this news, how he would feel, and how he would grieve alone behind bars without his family. I worried about my mother and couldn't help but think about the complicated grief of my Aunt Cat years ago — screaming her husband's name in the aftermath of his passing. I wept for them and with them. I asked for God's warring angels to put a hedge of peace and comfort over them all. After cancelling my appointments for the day, Anthony and I decided to drive two hours to tell Imani the news in person. We were concerned she would find out on social media, so we had to move fast. We had to be there to console and support her as the body language of immediate grief had its way with her too. The entire drive, I was numb. My face was flat, my stomach felt empty, and my heart was racing with anxiety. I prayed for God's strength and asked him to give me the words to articulate this news. *Sigh.*

This became a consistent theme in the early days of my grief. I was intensely aware of the gravity of sadness and sorrow this loss would have on my larger family and my entire hometown community who benefitted from my father's presence. He was dad. He was Poppy. He was Uncle Junie. He was Uncle Sam. He was Sam. He was Coach. He was fatherly. He was funny. He was smart. He was loving. He was a husband. He was a family man. He was a teacher. He was a mentor. He was a man's man. He was an all-around great guy. As my church sister, Elder Nneka wrapped it up, my dad was "everybody's everything" — which was easily confirmed in the tremendous outpouring on social media. It was as endearing as it was heartbreaking. Hundreds of students, athletes, coaches, teachers, family, and friends wrote personal testimonies, shared old photos, and reminisced with admiration about my dad. My Facebook notifications, texts, phone calls, bereavement cards, and flowers would not stop for weeks to come. The largeness of who he was, in the lives of so many, was quite apparent; which brought one pivotal thought to the forefront of my mind: *You would truly be hard-pressed to find anyone who has a negative, derogatory thing to say about* my father. What an amazing testament to his character. They were blessed just to know him.

In the aftermath of his passing, Anthony and I had been in heavy prayer and meditation about our personal grief, the grief of the immediate family, and the grief of the extended community of students, athletes, teachers, coaches, colleagues, and friends that were bereaved with us. I found myself drawn to the bible, Matthew 5: 4 *Blessed are those who mourn for they will be comforted.* I prayed and meditated on that scripture. It just kept nudging at me as I petitioned God to give me the words, to give me something, to lighten the hearts and minds of the hundreds of people in sorrow with me. In my prayers, he gave me a vision, which I delivered at his memorial ceremony.

An Excerpt from my speech at Dad's Funeral

PICTURE THIS: As we have been mourning together, God gave me a vision of the impassioned words from our mouths, the presence of our tears, our hugs, our shared memories, and our collective prayers being spiritually transformed into a string of thread or piece of fabric.

As we continue to speak well of my Father, and as we continue to keep my family lifted in prayer, we form hundreds of pieces of thread and fabric, which becomes spiritually transformed and interlocked together. So, when my cousin Randi shed some tears, and Michael Jenkins posted an endearing high school memory on Facebook, and because Danielle prayed with me over a Glide app, or because you lit a candle at the candlelight, or because you shared a photo...you too are forming a spiritual thread.

All of the pieces of thread form a massive, interlocking weave, a blanket, a comforter — a comforter that wraps us tight when we are sad, lonely, or grieving the loss of my father's presence here on earth. Perhaps it's the comforter that lifts you up when you're down because you hear his voice coaching you from the finish line saying — *"Go out and get it"* or *"Knees, knees, pump your arms, all the way through"*. This comforter encompasses my father's strong presence, his infectious smile, his unconditional regard, and all the special colloquialisms that only dad says, and it brings you to laughter. It turns your grief into comfort and gratitude because you got blessed just by knowing him, working alongside him, running or playing ball for him, or being loved or counseled by him. *Matthew 5:4 says Blessed are those who mourn for they will be comforted...* so you keep on mourning, and you keep on praying, and reminiscing, and posting on social media, and you keep on weaving more thread and fabric...because you are strengthening OUR comforter and blessing us all.

I returned to North Carolina the day after the funeral. As much as I wanted to stick around to comfort my mother, being a self-employed entrepreneur does not allow for paid bereavement leave or PTO. I went home with the initiative to return to Wednesday night worship service and to work the next day. Arriving home from the seven-hour drive, with an additional two-hour detour to return Imani to campus, I found myself completely worn out. I drove myself to the office, feeling like a ton of bricks—emotionally drained, unfocused, and stuck in my thoughts. Several clients cancelled appointments for the day and later through the week, which was all the push I needed to cancel them all. I used the next few days to breathe and returned to work on a modified schedule the following week.

Those early days of grief were an emotional rollercoaster. It seemed like I had an emotional tolerance of approximately fifty percent of its normal capacity, and when that tank ran empty, I was emotionally and physically exhausted. If I wanted to cry—I did. If I wanted to be alone—I went to my room and closed the door. If I was exhausted—I took a nap. I didn't force myself to do anything, merely following my instincts and allowing the emotions to come however they were going to come. Sometimes I was irritable over things that would not normally bother me. I could look at Dad's pictures one day feeling comforted and grateful—only to burst into tears the next day at the same picture. Sometimes I would drift off into my own thoughts. Sometimes my laughter would give way to tears. Other times, I could laugh and joke and feel as normal as I did before he died— which was confusing. *Was I supposed to be laughing?*

Before I answer this question, let me first explain that this bereavement period began just as Anthony and I agreed to declare a fast for ourselves. Fasting is a systematic detox throughout your body with fruits, vegetables, and natural grains, accompanied by a focused diligence for prayer and conversation with God. Sometimes fasting is nothing more than water; while other times, people will fast from specific things (like social media, cell phones, television) that serve as a distraction in your relationship with God. With both of our birthday's in September, we decided to fast for spiritual enlightenment and clarity in his professional direction to strengthen our family foundation. Our pastor then declared a corporate

> **Exodus 34:28**
> Moses was there with the LORD forty days and forty nights without eating bread or drinking water. And he wrote on the tablets the words of the covenant—the Ten Commandments.

fast for the entire church, which further elevated the spiritual process.

Now, here is what I deduced about whether I was supposed to be laughing during the grief process: My prayer request during the fasting period was for God to turn my grief into gratitude, so that when I had a heavy thought of sorrow and loss, missing my father; it would be overwhelmed and overshadowed by my gratitude for being a part of him. I have nothing but gratitude for him as a man, as a father, and as a grandfather. In my lifetime, he brought me far more laughter, love, and joy, then tears. Truth be told, you would be hard pressed to find anyone who had sorrowful, negative experiences with my father. *So was I supposed to be laughing – Yes*. Because that's what he and my mother raised me to do. One of my father's fOne of my father's favorite mantra's is an old African Proverb about lions and gazelles. It reads:

> *Every morning in Africa, a gazelle wakes up. It knows it must run faster than the fastest lion or it will be killed. Every morning in Africa, a lion wakes up. It knows it must outrun the slowest gazelle or it will starve to death. It doesn't matter whether you're a lion or a gazelle, when the sun comes up, you'd better be running.*

So, I know in my heart he would want me to keep running, keep living, and keep laughing. If he were still alive, he would likely say something borderline silly just to make me laugh—a role Anthony has fallen into since the day we met.

With that said, I am so convinced and deeply aware that God ordered my steps in the best way possible to go through this season of grief in an emotionally whole, unbroken way with a husband that will allow me to feel and be however I need to feel and be on that day. Then he will go grocery shopping, cook dinner, pick up the kids, walk the dog, and rub my back until I fall asleep. I am grateful. Thank you, God! Because if it had not been for the pull of God on my life several years ago, I would not be firmly planted under the covering of Have Life Church and my spiritual parents, Pastor Sho and Co-Pastor Jacque. They are profound leaders—the type of leaders that grow more amazing leaders for the kingdom of God and make peoples' lives better. Their leadership has had a marked impact on my spiritual and personal growth, and on the spiritual/personal growth of my husband. Before we met, Anthony and I were on individual paths of personal improvement—molded and shaped by our leaders to confront our indiscretions, past hurts, and ultimately get in alignment with God. Pastor and Co-Pastor raised us up to maturity in God, who ultimately drew Anthony and I together through Him. We are both firm believers that the God in him, fell in love with the God in me, and vice versa—allowing the order of things to happen how it is happening. It is not by accident. The definition of *coincidence* is rooted in Greek terminology from the word *synkyrian*, which is a combination of two words: *syn* meaning "together with" and *kurios* meaning "supreme in authority"[2]. So biblically speaking, coincidence is defined as *"what occurs together by God's providential arrangement of circumstances.[2]"* What appears to be random chance is in fact overseen by a sovereign God who directs the order of it all. If you believe things do not happen by accident, and that everything happens in the way that the Creator designs for it to happen—you can understand why I am so grateful and honored to raise up the name of God in this season of grief. I could still be single and brokenhearted and sleeping around, trying to find some sense of security and comfort. But I have a comforter—not only in my natural life with a husband, family, spiritual parents, and an awesome church family—but in my spiritual life as God, the Father. And now my natural-born father, is in heaven above with my heavenly Father, so I can draw comfort knowing that I am spiritually and naturally covered. Thank you, God! As if that is not enough, the bible is clear throughout scripture, stating God will turn your *mourning into joy, comfort you, and give you gladness for sorrow* (Isaiah 61:1-3, Jeremiah 31:13, John 16:20). Yes—laughter through the grief process is okay. Its evidence of his presence and his works in you.

[2] Beitman, Bernard. "If God is the Cause, There Are No Coincidences" posted April 23, 2017. Psychology Today <https://www.psychologytoday.com/blog/connecting-coincidence/201704/if-god-is-the-cause-there-are-no-coincidences>

Dr. Melissa Tate-Scruse

The Comforter

In some of the more challenging times of grief, I turned to Co-Pastor Jacque for support. I talked with her about the experience of speaking at my dad's funeral, and the spiritual "comforter" vision that downloaded through my prayers and meditation. She said, *"Melissa, I see clearly that this is your next book. Do some research on how a comforter is made and see what you find."* A quick Google search, and memories of sewing with my mother as a child, revealed a simple list of supplies and instructions — but in the vein of spiritual vision, it spoke to me.

Making a Comforter
2 pieces of fabric...................*Two people*
Sewing Machine/Kit.........*Prayer, The Word of God*
Batting or filling..................*The Holy Spirit*

Instructions:
When making a comforter, put two pieces of fabric together with the inner side (or printed side) facing each other. Sew along three sides of the perimeter, leaving the fourth side open (like a pillow case). Then turn it inside out so the patterned fabric is on the outside. Fill with batting/filling before stitching the fourth seam closed.

I was instantly reminded of scripture, *Matthew 18: 21 "For where two or three are gathered together in My name, I am there in the midst of them.* When people come together in prayer, they are bringing their insides together—their feelings, their vulnerabilities, their worries, their emotions. Imagine two or more people, perhaps hand in hand, standing together in prayer, pouring their insides-out of grief and sadness. The word of God is the sewing machine—providing the thread that acts like a sealant or bonding agent—to hold it all together and evokes the presence of The Holy Spirit. Biblically speaking, the Holy Spirit is the Comforter or Helper, sent by God as the third entity of the Holy Trinity (The Father, The Son, and The Holy Spirit). This is such a powerful analogy for communal prayer and support to provide comfort through the grieving process. My church family, who did not know my father from Adam, was essential to my grieving process.   As I returned home to North Carolina, separate from those who could identify most closely with my grief, there were certainly the customary and much appreciated hugs, cards, flowers, and condolences shared—but some people *gathered* with me and my family in prayer. And the healing comfort was there.

Relationship Status—*Married*
Emotional Status—*Grieving*
Mindset—*Blessed*.

Conclusion

Blessed Passenger

The title and concept for this book began several months before my father's passing. It was initially conceptualized to be a discussion of the grieving process in the aftermath of separation and divorce and the journey toward personal growth and spiritual maturity. I recall taking time off work in the early summer, just to dive into the writing process. I was sure to make a substantial dent in the framework of the book, but I got stuck writing about grief. When Anthony got home from work on day two of my week off, he said "How's it coming along?" I told him I thought I would have been further along, "I could almost write a whole book about grief." Fast forward some months later and I lose one of the most important people in my life. It's one thing to write about episodes of grief when you are years removed from the hurt and pain — but I've been writing the closing chapters of this book with fresh vulnerability and sadness. It has been an emotional rollercoaster — not the *Blind Passenger*, toxic relationships, bitter, resentful, emotional rollercoaster of my past. Despite bouts of heavy sadness and grief, this emotional rollercoaster has been a blessing. I find comfort knowing God is in control of it all. I don't have to fret or try to fix anything or be ashamed, because every tear, every experience, every moment of grief, every memory of nostalgic happiness, and every dream that I have had in the aftermath of my father's death has been one of enlightenment. Here's what I've found:

Defining Grief

Although grief is formally described as a deep sorrow associated with death; grief also transcends death to include reactions to loss of all kinds.

- Physical loss, i.e. death of a loved one or destroyed property
- Environmental loss, i.e. moving, relocation, natural disasters that destroy the community
- Social loss, i.e. separation, divorce, intimate breakups, changing schools, being fired from employment

Romantic breakups also carry grief.

Think about it: You must have loved, embraced, believed in, and found value in someone or something before you can grieve its loss or absence. If you never loved it, believed in it, or found value in it, its absence would be no big deal. Its absence would have little to no impact on you, your thoughts, or your mind. In this respect, to understand the experience of grief and to truly process the various losses we experience in our lives, you must first process the experience of love.

I believe we use the term, LOVE, rather loosely in this modern day. We love our shoes. We love our phones. We love our favorite TV shows. We are programmed to love what's hot and new and exciting. We love, we love, we love. Romantically, we "fall in love" so quickly believing that people are our soul mates and that we'll love them forever. We give people unquantifiable value in our lives—it's so romantic, often indescribable, and intangible... *"I can't describe it, I just love him."* But the truth is we don't necessarily love the person—we love the way we feel when we are with a person. Their presence makes you feel something, experience something, believe something; and that's what you fall in love with. We fall in love with the experiences we have had with a person, the feelings that are prevalent when that person is near, and the belief that this person is the only one who can cultivate it. When you love someone, you're giving power, value, substance, and purpose to them, and you're assigning them to be that purpose in your life.

But when that love is set on fire, when the experiences and feelings change, when it doesn't quite feel the same, when the nearness is taken away or even believed to be fading—grief sets in. The love is set on fire and we become emotionally affected by the heartbreak, the fading presence and "loss" of love, feeling incomplete without them near. Something is missing, life feels different, and you'll fight with desperation to get it back. You just want to put out the fire. This is often why people stay in dead-end relationships. We are often fighting with desperation to restore what once was, even when it was only designed to be a temporary "situation-ship." Or you are fighting to keep up with the idea of "love" you have in your head—which usually unrealistic and unreachable based on present evidence. And sometimes, we work overtime in attempt to restore what the relationship used to be. In all reality, some relationships need to die. Some people in our lives have been given too much power, credit, and value; and that false assignment of love, that obsession, that toxic belief needs to die in order for you to realize and develop your own sense of power, credit, and value. Once you have your own sense of power, credit, and value; the absence of the person is no longer considered a loss. In the case of my past toxic relationships, I was more than agreeable to divorce and reevaluate my life separate from the unhealthy behaviors; but that had an impact on every other area of my life.

Grief and relief go hand in hand.

Whether you are going through a loss or life change related to separation, divorce, relocation, breakup, or death, it is common to go through a dual emotional experience of grief and relief. You can have heavy feelings of sadness and loneliness about a recent breakup, yet still find some sense of relief knowing the arguments or the cheating or mistrust is over. You can have feelings of anger that your job did not give you a raise or respect your efforts, thus prompting you to secure a new job; and at the same time, feel a sense of relief that you don't have to face the stress of overworking yourself to prove your value. In the case of premature death, perhaps your loved one had a wayward lifestyle of drugs, alcohol, and legal issues. Although saddened and grieving the loss, you may also have some sense of peace knowing they are no longer fighting addiction. With my father's death, I have a sense of relief knowing there will be no more blood sugar checks, insulin injections, kidney failure, cholesterol problems, doctor's appointments, etc.; yet I am always and forever a daddy's girl, missing him and mourning his absence just the same.

It is the experience of grief, sadness, and sorrow that can keep you stuck in your thoughts and/or stagnant in your lifestyle. In the aftermath of a break up or radical life change, I encourage you to fuel and refocus on the RELIEF experience, as reviewed in Chapter 2. What are your plans to bring a sense of relief and peace of mind to your life?

- ✓ REALITY_____
- ✓ EMOTIONAL COMPOSURE_____
- ✓ LONELINESS VS ALONENESS_____
- ✓ INVEST IN YOU _____
- ✓ EDUCATION_____
- ✓ FUTURE_____

These factors are focused on rebuilding your Individual Identity and sense of self, as other areas of your life are in flux because of the loss. Particularly in the aftermath of toxic, unhealthy relationships, the Individual Identity has suffered for the sake of the relationship. Completing a self-defining exercise such as this can help you look beyond your current circumstance and plan for your future accordingly. What are your financial goals? Are you where you want to be in your career? Do you need to return to school? How is your health? Do you have any goals for exercise or eating habits you've not been disciplined about? Now is the time, to reset your focus on you.

Use this chart as a platform to set goals for the upcoming months using a SMART Goal guideline: S-Specific, M-Measurable, A-Attainable, R-Realistic and T-Timely.

GOAL	DATE TO ACCOMPLISH GOAL BY:

What do I need to accomplish my goal?

(Skills, Education, Career Advancement or Change, Finances, Resources, etc.,)

What actions do I need to take to accomplish my goal? Be Specific – Ex: I need to earn $5000)	**Steps required to complete the action.** How? – Ex: Secure a PT job, Increase my sales, etc.)
Who can I share my goals with to keep me accountable and on track? Identify 3 people who will challenge and support you with your goals	

*A*fter losing a loved one, I encourage counseling and bereavement support to process the wealth of emotions related to the death. There are times when people shy away from looking at pictures and memorabilia, but I have found it helpful. When my Aunt Cat passed away, pictures helped me re-shift my thoughts from the near-unrecognizable medical compromise she was in before her passing; and with dad's death, the picture slide show that KJ and I composed for his memorial service, as well as all the social media dedications, was as therapeutic as it was endearing. It kept his lively spirit fresh on my mind. Lastly, spiritual reading, prayer, and meditation has been critical to my grief process. Studying Jesus' explanation of his forthcoming death as the disciples began to grasp considering a life without his presence helped ground my spiritual understanding of life and death. The revelation and relief I've received from the word of God has been comforting through one of the toughest times of my life.

Grieving Alone vs. Grieving Collectively

When an entire family, community, church, or organization is collectively experiencing the loss of a beloved member, it multiplies the gravity of the grieving event. If a hurricane or tornado sweeps through a specific geographic region, the whole community is impacted by death, injury, weather-beaten homes, a shortage of resources, and a weakened infrastructure for recovery. Everyone in the area is collectively grieving the losses, sometimes weighing each other down in the process. This is often why people are encouraged to abandon the area to fortify a sense of structure in a safe location. When working at the RTC, there were easily two hundred people — students and staff — affected by the suicide of one student. It left an emotional wound exposed for several weeks and months thereafter, as it was constantly a part of people's experience of trauma throughout the building, i.e. *remember when*…or *things have been different since*…or *I heard*. With my father's passing, his profound impact on the educational and athletic community in our hometown has left a void. His presence was well received and respected, therefore his absence is difficult. Standing in front of hundreds in the stadium bleachers, I could see their teary eyes, saddened faces, and heavy hearts on their sleeves. My grief as an individual person, mourning the death of my father, was multiplied by the hundreds of grieving faces before me.

Upon my return to North Carolina after the funeral arrangements, outside of my husband and children, everyone who was grieving with me had retreated to their corner of the world to deal with the grief on their own. I believe this is when the long-term process of grief begins to take root. It's the attempt to resume normalcy when something doesn't quite seem normal. It's their name in your cell phone. It's the time of day you might typically call him, but he's not there to call. It's the voicemail that has their voice on it. It's dealing with the "business side" of death, including death certificates and ashes and insurance claims and leftover assets/debts. You are barely a week or even a month removed from their passing, but you must make these big decisions through your anguish and sadness. For me, it was walking into my parents' guest bedroom cleaning up his belongings, knowing he wouldn't visit anymore.

Once you get through this phase of daily routine, perhaps you're less tearful and things are beginning to feel somewhat normal. Someone who knows your loved one calls or visits you; and their grief makes your grief bubble up to the surface. Or perhaps a holiday or birthday is approaching, and you are faced with the reality that they won't be there for the family gathering. I had a mini-crying spell when discussing who will make the cornbread at Thanksgiving—Dad always makes the cornbread. From scratch. And it's delicious. I just wanted to shout, NO MORE CORNBREAD EVER! This is the process. It's a bruise that never quite heals to 100 percent.

So, is it better to grieve alone or together? In the aftermath of a death or a breakup, I think it's appropriate to retreat to your private sanctuary to feel however you need to feel. If there are no imminent safety concerns, we all need time to be alone with our thoughts and perhaps have a good cry, or two. If crying spells and isolation turns into repeated days of darkness, not eating, not talking; then it's time to shift to grieving together. It is important to get connected with someone or something that gives you a sense of purpose and life energy. For me, it's God, family, and church.   My candid conversations with God, dreams he has given me, and revelation that has downloaded from my prayers has been empowering. Spending time with my family, forming more life memories and experiences has kept me laughing. Serving at Have Life Church is such a joy. I've poured out my tears in that church. I've been on my knees in prayer in that church. And I have celebrated life in that church. These things are all a part of my life purpose and give me *life energy*. When I need to have a good, open-hearted conversation about how much I thought of Dad today, I call my mother or talk with my husband. If I come across a picture or thought that warms my heart, I share it. I am confident I will never grieve alone, even if I'm grieving separately from others.

As a therapist, I have a greater emotional intelligence and understanding than most.   I can recognize my feelings as they come to the surface — sadness, repressed agitation, irritability, guilt. *Grief comes in waves*, they say; but sometimes it's one of those wipeout-type of waves that you don't see coming. About a month after my father passed away, a good friend of mine also lost her father. She came up to me at church, asking with great passion and curiosity, *"How are you doing this?"* I was able to have a very poignant, pleasant conversation with her about letting my emotions happen as they needed to happen—not bottling them up, allowing myself to shed a tear, and allowing myself to smile or laugh or reminisce. I wasn't expecting her to approach me that morning, and I managed the conversation quite well, but it must have poked a hole in my emotional tank. Through the remainder of the day, I kept thinking about my dad and that conversation. I kept it moving, staying busy with the daily routine. By the end of the night, I was tired and had been getting increasingly agitated over the slightest things. As Anthony and I were remodeling Gizele's bedroom, I hit the roof, yelling about mattresses, sheets, and matching pillows. They were looking at me like I was crazy, which, in all honesty, made me even madder. *Wipeout*! In retrospect, even though I had a legitimate gripe about the mattresses, sheets, and pillows, my response was so extra out of character. I'm generally the easy breezy one, but it's safe to say my earlier conversation spilled over throughout the day. It happens.

Grieving is a spiritual journey.

Every loss and significant life transition I have experienced has prompted a period of self-reflection that cultivated change in my life direction. It wasn't until writing this book that I realized there is some connection between my various seasons of grief and spiritual renewal. It is as if the natural order of the world forces something to die—either an actual death or a subjective death to marriage, job, etc.—before something else can be birthed. We often adhere to popular expressions like, *"when one door closes, another door opens"* or *"out with the old, in with the new";* which ultimately validates grief, loss, and significant life transitions as a spiritual cleansing process. Loss forces you to birth a new way of being outside of what you are accustomed to.

I'm a firm believer that God will sometimes force you to a position of discomfort in order to provoke change in your life, to renew your mind beyond what you are used to and grow you into different areas of purpose and understanding. At times, we are so focused on our wants, trying to "fix" things that are beyond our fixing. We want the relationship to last. We want the promotion at work because we believe we deserve it. We weren't ready for our loved one to pass away. We were unprepared for the hurricane or blizzard. Sometimes it just doesn't seem fair that various crises are piling up around us, and we turn our anger to self, others, doctors, Mother Nature, and even God—asking *"How could You let this happen?"* People tend to become angry with God thinking He has abandoned, betrayed, mistreated them, or allowed something terrible to happen[3]. In his book, *The*

---

[3] Ekstrand, D.W. "Dealing With Anger Toward God" The Transformed Soul at
http://www.thetransformedsoul.com/additional-studies/spiritual-life-studies/dealing-with-anger-toward-god

Dr. Melissa Tate-Scruse

Transformed Soul, Dr. D.W. Ekstrand, a renowned theologian, pastor, and biblical scholar, wrote about "Dealing With Anger Toward God":

> When some extreme difficulty or tragedy happens in our lives, we naturally ask God the question — "Why?" This response indicates two flaws in our thinking — first, even as believers we all have the tendency to operate under the impression that life should be easy and pleasant (especially if GOD is our God), and that God should prevent tragedy, difficulty and pain from happening to us (John 11:37); so when He does not, we get angry or disappointed with Him (John 11:32). Second, when we do not seem to be able to reconcile the extent of God's sovereignty, we lose confidence in His ability to control all of the circumstances we go through in life. When we lose faith in God's sovereignty, it is actually because our frail human flesh is grappling with our own frustration and our own lack of control over events. All of us tend to live life in such a way that we can positively affect the outcome of situations…that everything will work out as we planned; as such, we believe that we are the ones who ultimately determine our fate — when good things happen, we generally attribute it to our own efforts; so when things go bad we are quick to blame God, and get angry with Him for not preventing it. Deep down we

believe we should be immune to unpleasant circumstances...especially if God loves us. (n.p)

Here is the bottom line: Life is not always fair. Everything is designed to happen in its time and you are not privileged to know it all in advance. Ecclesiastes 3: 1-8, 11 (NKJV) reads:

> To everything there is a season, A time for every purpose under heaven; A time to be born, And a time to die; A time to plant, And a time to pluck what is planted; A time to kill, And a time to heal; A time to break down, And a time to build up; A time to weep, and a time to laugh; A time to mourn, And a time to dance; A time to cast away stones; A time to embrace, And a time to refrain from embracing; A time to gain, And a time to lose; A time to keep, And a time to throw away; A time to tear, And a time to sew, A time to keep silence, and a time to speak; A time to love, And a time to hate; A time of war, and at time of peace. He has made everything beautiful in its time. Also, He has put eternity in their hearts except that no one can find out the work that God does from beginning to end.

Having a steady walk with God through difficult seasons of grief has kept me grounded in the natural and spiritual order of the world we live in. It doesn't mean I don't get upset or get tripped up in my feelings—I'm still human. But when *(not if)* adversity comes, my faith and belief in God keeps my feet on the ground and my emotions in check.

Dr. Melissa Tate-Scruse

When my father passed away, it was as if a spiritual portal opened within me. Visions have been downloading into my spirit while I am in prayer and meditation. I have been having intense dreams of spiritual significance. I've been awakened from my sleep, drawn to certain scriptures or to pray about specific things and people. I believe my father's protective, loving spirit has transcended in heaven to guide me. Psalm 91:11 reads *"For He shall give His angels charge over you, To keep you in all your ways."* There is no doubt in my mind that he is with me.

My Mantras for Bereavement: You'd Better Be's

You'd Better Be Running—
derived from my father's favorite African Proverb

Every morning in Africa, a gazelle wakes up. It knows it must run faster than the fastest lion or it will be killed. Every morning in Africa, a lion wakes up. It knows it must outrun the slowest gazelle or it will starve to death. It doesn't matter whether you're a lion or a gazelle, when the sun comes up, you'd better be running. Everything about grief, mourning, and bereavement makes you want to slow down and curl up in bed. You feel shocked, numb, sad, heavy, tired, and sometimes angry. You're stuck in an altered state of mind as you begin to fathom the world without your loved one. Although, this is an appropriate reaction in the grief process, it is also an opportunity for prolonged bouts of depression, anxiety, impulsive sexuality, substance abuse, and other health issues to take root. Because of your vulnerable state, these things will try to find a home in your mind and body. John 10:10a (NLT) says, "*The thief's purpose is to steal kill and destroy...*" In this respect, your grieving heart is the perfect playground for additional negativity and stress to weigh you down and get the best of you. If you have previously struggled in the grieving process, have had difficulties with your health, or have a history of psychiatric or substance abuse disorders, the likelihood of relapse and complicated grief may be intensified. Be mindful of what and who you allow in your life while you are grieving. Surround yourself with proper support, medicine, doctors, loved ones—those that will keep you in healthy *running* order and not allow the grief to overburden you. The world around you is moving at its *normal* pace with *normal* expectations and deadlines. Returning to your fully functioning-self will be difficult, so take your

> *Grief is not a sprint, it's a marathon. Pace yourself but keep on running.*

time. Be honest about your difficulties, allow yourself to struggle, and pace yourself to do a little more each day. It is not a sprint (grief is not quick and easy) …it's a marathon, but *you'd better be running*.

You'd Better Be Mourning —
derived from Matthew 5:4

"Blessed are those who mourn, for they will be comforted." In its biblical context, this scripture pertains to a person's grief related to their sins and desire for repentance. But in my prayer time, it resonated so heavily with me and brought vision to the collective burden of grief I was carrying for my extended family and hometown. I saw the tears, warm thoughts, stories, pictures, and good tidings spoken over my father spiritually transformed into yards of thread, forming a comforter. It blessed me to know the active process of mourning — the tears, conversations, memories, etc. — evokes the spiritual presence of physical and emotional comfort. In this respect, the more we mourn and grieve the life of our loved one, the stronger our comforter becomes — giving warmth, revelation, and joy. He turns our mourning into joy…so, *you'd better be mourning*.

Eckhart Tolle, a world-renowned spiritual teacher and author, compassionately explains the internal conflict that can arise as you reach a spiritual deepening in your grieving process:

> The natural way of being after the death of a loved one is suffering at first, then there is a deepening.

In that deepening, you go to a place where there is no death…. Conditioned as your mind is by society, the contemporary world that you live in…tells you that there is something wrong with this. Your mind says, 'I should not be feeling peace, that is not what one feels in a situation like this.' But that's a conditioned thought [or programmed thought] by the culture you live in. So instead…recognize it as a conditioned thought that is not true. It doesn't mean the waves of sadness don't come back from time to time. But in between the waves of sadness, you sense there is peace. As you sense that peace, you sense the essence of [your loved one] as well — the timeless essence. So, death is a very sacred thing — not just a dreadful thing.[4]

Grieving my father's death has been an enlightening spiritual opportunity. It has brought me vision and clarity, and yes peace amidst the sadness. It warms my heart to continue hearing of various forms of tribute to his honor. I recently received photos of the Oakland Mills High School track team, where he spent the bulk of his career, donning his initials on their uniform sleeve. This collective grief and mourning process continues to bring joy and peace in my heart.

---

[4] Tolle, Eckhart. September 2011 Newsletter: "Eckhart on Peace After a Loss." Retrieved on April 24, 2018 at www.eckharttolle.com/newslettter/september-2011/

Dr. Melissa Tate-Scruse

You'd Better Be Gathering –

Founded in Matthew 18: 21

"For where two or three are gathered together in My name, I am there in the midst of them." When people gather in the name of Jesus, He shows up! Jesus is the ultimate, true example of love. At a time of mourning, you need some people who will show you love and *gather* with you. I thank God for blessing me with friends and loved ones who know how to gather. They know how to pick up the phone as soon as they hear the news and they weep, cry, or sit in silence with you. Gatherers are the people who show up at your front door just to hug on you and see your face. They sit on the front pew with you before the funeral begins, just to hold your hand and comfort you. Sometimes you haven't seen your best gatherers in 5, 10, or 20 years, but they buy plane tickets and take extended road trips just to be at the memorial services. They travel across town or multiple states just to show their love. Some gatherers are not your everyday besties, but they wrap their arms around you and slide a love offering in your hand "for you and only you." I had some gatherers send poems, heartfelt messages, and greeting cards with handwritten notes. I have been blessed with the type of gatherers that send food to your front door, so you don't have to worry about cooking. And last, but certainly not least, my gatherers are prayer warriors who drop down on their knees before God. They lay their hands on you

in spiritual agreement, and they send angels of peace, restoration, and comfort to your grieving heart. If you are not a prayer warrior, you ought to know someone who is because there is healing and comfort in the name of Jesus. There is nothing more special than someone who will have a conversation with God on behalf of your grieving heart. At a time of mourning, *you'd better be gathering*.

> *There is nothing more special than someone who will have a conversation with God on behalf of your grieving heart.*
>
> -Dr. Melissa-

Jesus Teaches about Death and Grief

Before Jesus was crucified, he met with the disciples teaching them about grief in anticipation of his death — John 16 (NIV). Studying this scripture helped me put death and bereavement in perspective. I pray it blesses your understanding as well.

To everything there is a season, A time for every purpose under heaven; A time to be born, And a time to die; A time to plant, And a time to pluck what is planted; A time to kill, And a time to heal; A time to break down, And a time to build up; A time to weep, and a time to laugh; A time to mourn, And a time to dance; A time to cast away stones; A time to embrace, And a time to refrain from embracing; A time to gain, And a time to lose; A time to keep, And a time to throw away; A time to tear, And a time to sew, A time to keep silence, and a time to speak; A time to love, And a time to hate; A time of war, and at time of peace. He has made everything beautiful in its time. Also, He has put eternity in their hearts except that no one can find out the work that God does from beginning to end.

- **4b "Because I was with you"**

At times we are in the flesh, in the natural world, with people and do not get all the time and information we need or want from them. We sometimes take their presence for granted thinking they will always be there, and we get comfortable with the accessibility of their presence.

- **5 But now I am going to him who sent me."**

When we die, we return to our heavenly father. He is the Creator of all and he put us in earthly presence for our time. At some point, he brings you back.

- 6 "You are filled with grief because I said these things"

An instant feeling of loss and sadness overwhelms the disciples as they begin to consider their lives without the physical presence of Jesus. I imagine, the body language of grief taking over them—shock, bewilderment, perhaps tearfulness with flattened expressions, numbness. As Jesus is talking, I imagine them thinking of all the miracles he has performed and teaching he has given them—everything they've learned from him.

- 7 "But very truly I tell you, it is for your good that I am going away. Unless I go away, the Advocate [the Comforter/the Helper] will not come to you, but if I go, I will send him to you…10b because I am going to the Father, where you can see me no longer…16 Jesus went on to say, "in a little while you will see me no more, and then after a little while you will see me."

When someone passes away, the loss of their physical presence allows the gift of the spirit, their spiritual presence to come to you. The endearing loss on earth transcends all space and time and allows a spiritual seed/a spiritual helper to come to you. You can no longer physically see the person in their earthen state, but if you hold fast to your spiritual awareness, you will see, feel, and experience them again. The thought of death brings confusion—whether it is a sudden unexpected loss or a

terminal condition that has led to an approaching loss —
we question why it has occurred. We ponder whether
something more can be done, and we consider all of the
"shoulda, coulda, woulda's and *what ifs"* that keep us stuck
in confusion, anguish, and sometimes guilt.

- **20 Very truly I tell you, you will weep and
  mourn...You will grieve, but your grief will turn
  to joy. 21 A woman giving birth to a child has
  pain because her time has come; but when her
  baby is born she forgets the anguish because of
  her joy that a child is born unto the world. 22 So
  with you: Now is your time of grief, but I will
  see you again and you will rejoice, and no one
  will take away your joy."**

Grief, weeping, and mourning will turn to irrevocable joy
if you allow the spirit of those who have died to comfort
you. Allow the joy and goodness they are and have been
to you to overpower your sadness and grief. That joy
cannot be taken from you. That joy opens your spiritual
eyes and allows you to "see" and feel that loved one. And
that joy is yours to have.

- **33 "I have told you these things, so that in me you
  may have peace. In this world you will have
  trouble. But take heart! I have overcome the
  world."**

Death is an overcoming of the natural world and all of the troubles within it. Regardless of how one spends their life on this earth—philanthropist, drug dealer, school teacher, chef, alcoholic, fighting cancer, athlete, criminal, it doesn't matter—at the moment of death, with confession and sincere belief that He is Lord, we all have the capacity to overcome this world. We are forgiven, justified, and cleared of all guilt and condemnation by faith in Christ. Everyone who calls on the name of the Lord will be saved. There is relief. They have peace, which we need to take to heart and allow ourselves peace from grief.

I n the final stages of concluding this book, I woke up in the middle of the night, restless for seemingly no reason. I did not necessarily feel called to pray or do anything in particular, but I was restless nonetheless. After tossing, turning, drinking some water, and thinking about a random list of things—laundry, my kids, my scheduled appointments for tomorrow, etc.—my thoughts wandered to my father. I began thinking about a recent conversation between my mother and one of his doctors. She was told that my father lived ten years longer than he was supposed to in spite of the rigorous, prolonged nature of his diabetic condition. I have thought about this idea before. My brother, KJ, actually mentioned it during his eulogy at the funeral; but on this night, the gravity of this idea overwhelmed me.

Let me explain: Approximately ten years ago, my father's diabetes had taken a severe toll on him. He was in full renal failure, going through dialysis several days a week, and had been placed on the donor's list for a kidney and a pancreas. I was given this news, just after discovering my pregnancy with Erin. I was horrified at the thought of possibly being a "match" to donate a kidney to my father, yet unable to participate in the testing process because of my pregnancy. In God's will, KJ was a perfect match. In the summer of 2006, the two men I hold so dear, were admitted to Johns Hopkins Hospital for a successful kidney transplant procedure. It could have been another way, but God allowed us ten more years with my father.

As I laid in bed, pondering the last ten years, I began to weep tears of joy for all that it brought. *God used my brother as a life vessel to gift my father 10 more years with us.* This allowed him to be present for our respective marriages, the birth of three out of four biological grandchildren—two of whom he watched compete with national success in dance and outdoor track. KJ and I had doctoral graduations, and Imani graduated high school to transition to collegiate sports/academia. Dad gave me away in my marriage to Anthony and grew to love three more granddaughters. In those last ten years, we enjoyed family vacations to Disney World and various beaches along the Carolina Coast. He was gifted 10 more years alongside his soul mate and life partner—retired, visiting casinos, and traveling to see family in various states. In the perspective of life and death, this is truly a gift. I have prayed for God to have my grief overshadowed with gratitude, and he keeps showing out! It's such a blessing to see His hands on it all, to look back over life's milestones and see his *Footprints* in the sand.

In my joyful mourning, I pray the blessings of the Lord over my brother:

> *Heavenly Father, you are so amazing. You are a masterful creator, a strong tower, a never-failing help, a warming comfort, a merciful healer, a deliverer – you are everything to me. I honor you, I lift your name on high, and I thank you for being God. Thank you for putting KJ on my heart at this time. I pray the blessings of the Lord never grow weary of falling on him. I pray for his abundant capacity to be used as a vessel for Gods glory. I pray his ability to stand in the gap and extend a lifeline to others never falters. I pray for his health and resilience through the length of his days. May the 10 years that he extended to our father be returned to him, blessed and multiplied more abundantly. May the generational impact of fatherhood and family togetherness that has been birthed in him never come under the attack of the enemy; that a beacon of love and protection always settle in his relationships with his wife and sons, to transcend his days on this earth. I thank you God, for allowing me to bear witness to and be a receiver of his goodness. He has been an amazing*

Dr. Melissa Tate-Scruse

teacher, support, friend, playmate, and role mode over the years — all that a sister could ask for. May I never take his presence or brotherly love for granted.

In Jesus name I pray, Amen.

Blessed Passenger

Artwork: A. Scruse

"She was no longer wrestling
with the grief but could sit down
with it as a lasting companion
and make it a sharer in her thoughts."
-George Eliot-

Acknowledgements

Thank you, God,
for your ever-faithful covering. There aren't enough
words to express how grateful I am for Your
presence. I honor You. I give You all the glory. And
I will always lift Your name in praise!

Anthony—You are my best friend,
my kingdom mate, my homie-lover-friend, and
more. I thank God for ordering our steps together.
There's no other person I could imagine walking
through this life with.
I choose you, again and again and again.

Imani, Gizelle, Janese, Ann, and Erin—
My 5 bubblin' brown beauties, individually and
collectively you have filled our home with lots of
love, laughter, and personality.
It's never a dull moment.
To my 3 Scruse babies,
thank you for trusting me and for sharing your dad
with me and your sisters.

Mother Dear, KJ, and Pure—we are in this one together, feeling it differently, or perhaps just the same, but together nonetheless. You each mean so much to me. Thank you for your continued love and support and for loving the girls and I through the journey.

Pastor Shomari and Copastor Jacque White,
You are amazing leaders with sincere hearts of gold. Thank you for pouring into me, challenging me, and growing me up in Christ.
Your spiritual love and support is unfailing. You are true examples of LOVING IN AWE—making everyone's life better.

To My "Gatherers,"
Friends, family, loved ones—Please know that you each hold a special place in my heart.

A blessing of honorable mention goes out to *Sonja, Tracy, Brea, Danielle, Ms. Jan, Elder Tavia,* and *Deacon Donald.* From various walks of life and areas of expertise, you have aided this project with your prayers, insight, and feedback.
I'm beyond grateful for you.

I want to specifically mention two very tight-knit, loving, supportive communities. They grieved with me and for me, along with my entire family:

Have Life Church and **Oakland Mills**
in my hometown of Columbia, MD.

Church family—without knowing my father personally, you wrapped your arms around me,

Blessed Passenger

prayed with me, and supported me through one of the most challenging times of my life.

Oakland Mills, I thank you for the show of pride and hometown love in memorializing my father. It was such a bitter sweet affair, as he would've been excited to love, laugh, and catch up with all of you.
Big ol' smile, bright orange jacket…
I know he was there.

Lastly, to all the readers grieving a death, a break up, or a life changing situation:
There is RELIEF.
There is life and love after a failed relationship.
There is joy in the midst of your mourning.
There is a recipe of comfort to get you through.
There are *Footprints* in the sand.

God Bless Everyone!

Dr. Melissa Tate-Scruse

Angels by Richard Smallwood

Through danger seen and unseen

There's protection all around

Under the refuge of God's wings

Security is found

For there are angels watching you

to keep you in all of your ways

Keeping you from stumbling, so don't be afraid

God's appointed angels watching over me

Angels watching over me

* * * * * * *

Unseen hands, guiding me

Through my storm and through my rain

Healing hands holding me

Through the darkness of my pain

Wings of loving hands around me so I will not fear

For I can feel the presence covering me

Nothing but angels watching over me

Angels watching over me

* * * * * * *

This book was written in loving memory of my father.

Dr. Melissa Tate-Scruse

For Booking:
BlindPassenger2015@Gmail.com

Dr. Tate-Scruse is a Licensed Professional Counselor and Clinical Supervisor in the State of North Carolina with a Doctor of Education in Counseling Psychology. She has 13 years of experience working with emotionally disrupted  individuals, couples, and families. She has a passion for breaking down the stigma related to mental illness and mental health counseling.

In her book writing debut, **Blind Passenger**, Dr. Tate-Scruse shares some of her personal struggles with  toxic intimate relationships and family addiction. She initiates "necessary conversations" that aim to break generational patterns of domestic violence, alcoholism, substance abuse, and the emotional fallout of that unpredictable rollercoaster.

Blessed Passenger

In this follow up memoire, **Blessed Passenger** explores seasons of grief, loss, and radical life transition in the aftermath of separation and divorce. It is a testimony of increasing faith and spiritual transformation despite the aftershock of sorrow and anguish through life's most complicated ups and downs.

Are you looking for ...
A motivational speaker ?
A subject matter expert?
A mental health professional?
A trainer or teacher?
#Ask Dr. Melissa

For Booking:
BlindPassenger2015@Gmail.com
www.drmetate.com
Facebook@ Ms. MediTate & Mingle
Instagram @drmetate

98459305R00098

Made in the USA
Columbia, SC
25 June 2018